A NATION IN
CRISIS

G. L. Simpson

authorHOUSE·

AuthorHouse™
1663 Liberty Drive
Bloomington, IN 47403
www.authorhouse.com
Phone: 833-262-8899

Published by AuthorHouse 10/14/2021

ISBN: 978-1-6655-3915-9 (sc)
ISBN: 978-1-6655-3914-2 (e)

Print information available on the last page.

This book is printed on acid-free paper.

CONTENTS

CONTENTS

DEDICATION AND ACKNOWLEDGEMENTS

This book is dedicated to my loving parents, Harvey A. and Lennie Echols Simpson, who taught us the value of honesty, hard work and a loving family.

I am grateful to my younger brothers, Fred C. and Claude Simpson, for their help in providing valuable quotations and Biblical research.

To my older brother Leonard, for a lifetime of brotherly inspiration.

For the Biblical and Historical research done by so many scholars and historians throughout time, and to the many loving teachers who made so much of this knowledge available to me in my lifetime, I am very grateful.

Although the ideals and beliefs expressed in this book illustrate how I strongly feel, they are also the feelings of many Americans throughout our history and I am grateful to them for making their thoughts known to us.

FOREWORD

This writing is blunt and to the point, perhaps harsh in the eyes of some, so anyone with a weak stomach, anyone who is weak-kneed or spineless, probably should not read further.

It offers some history (sorely lacking today), some skepticism and ridicule, a little fatherly advice and a large amount of fear and concern for the future of this great land called America and the American people.

This is an attempt to express my thoughts and beliefs based on more than three-quarters of a century of observing what goes on in the world, especially the actions of what can be called "the enemy within", and considerable research.

It is hoped that these words will, at least, cause some people to think about the state of our nation, ask questions and demand leaders who truly care about the country and the American people, not just their own selfish interest.

All opinions expressed herein, good or bad, are my own, after considerable research.

Warning: *"This writing could cause some people, who have blindly followed or believed in the doctrines or teachings of the liberals, to question or rethink those teachings".*

PROLOGUE

"America, love it or leave it"

For a lot of years now I have felt that many Americans no longer love our country. It's hard to say if they don't love our nation or have just become complacent and lazy. You see so few places, homes and businesses, that still fly the American flag.

Over forty years ago I made the observation that most Americans are just too comfortable. If a problem doesn't affect them directly, in a serious and uncomfortable way, they just don't seem to care. So often, when they do see a problem, you hear them say "someone should do something about that". As though they are not *someone*.

It seems that most people could be put in a long line, side-by-side, with someone going down the line hitting each one with a club, and most would not say or do anything until he gets to them. They would hope the assailant would get tired or break the stick. As the saying goes; "just don't take away my cold beer and my TV remote".

How many people do you know who call or write to their representatives? or write to their local newspaper to voice their opinion on important matters?

No doubt most Americans would be hard pressed to tell you the names of their political "leaders" and even less likely to know where those office-holders stand on the most important issues or how they are voting on those issues. Thomas Jefferson said *"If we are to guard against ignorance and remain free, it is the responsibility of every American to be informed"*.

So often we hear people say "I am only one person; what can I do?" Or they say "my one vote won't make a difference." They don't realize that by adding their one voice to a hundred or a thousand other "one voices" can make a difference. That many voices can get the attention of most politicians. Especially at election time. Elections have been decided by one vote.

Today many people rely on the major networks, national news, for almost all information. If they don't see it on their favorite network, it doesn't exist. If they do see it on their channel, no matter how false or incorrect, they take it as gospel truth. They don't care to research the matter and find the true facts.

People don't realize, the major news agencies are the greatest tools of the left-wing socialists, bent on taking down our country.

With news media, daytime soaps and late night, would-be comedians, TV has caused more brain damage than a pandemic of encephalitis.

As old time cowboy humorist, Will Rogers, said; *"how do you know when a politician is lying? His lips are moving."*

"*I pledge allegiance to the Flag of the United States of America, and to the Republic for which it stands, one Nation under **God**, indivisible, with liberty and justice for all.*"

"*The U.S. Flag, adapted on June 14, 1777, is the fourth oldest national flag in the world. The oldest being Denmark's flag, adapted in 1219.*"

"*Our National Anthem was written in 1814 by Francis Scott Key, during the War of 1812. It was set to music by a church organist, John Stafford Smith. The U.S. Navy started using the song in 1889. Congress passed a resolution making it our National Anthem in 1931. It was signed into law by President Herbert Hoover.*"

HISTORY – A BRIEF REVIEW

"We must indeed, all hang together, or most assuredly, we shall all hang separately" Benjamin Franklin

For the somewhat older American this can be considered a review, or reminder, of things we were taught in our earlier years when history and geography were considered important subjects. For some of us, the days of the simple two-room schoolhouse.

For the younger reader, who might not have been given the opportunity or privilege of learning how our nation was formed and what the cost was for so many of our founding fathers, it is hoped that this short history will spark an interest in learning more.

It took a lot of years and tremendous sacrifice for America to become a nation from the time when Christopher Columbus first discovered her by accident, while searching for a shorter trade route to Asia in 1492. It took almost three hundred years for it to become an independent nation. After a considerable amount of fighting, suffering and dying.

The people who settled in the new world that came to

be known as America were, for the most part, courageous individuals. Perhaps some could be called adventure seekers but most were people who could no longer tolerate cruel, oppressive rulers. They were willing to abandon what had been their homeland, and many relatives and friends, in hopes of finding a better life for themselves and their families. To find these freedoms they were willing to risk everything, to cross a vast ocean in rather crude sailing vessels, to an uncharted wilderness where, only God knew what awaited them.

These early revolutionaries were well aware of the bad side of a thing called human nature. The selfishness, greed and weaknesses of mankind. They and their fellowmen had been ruled and abused by kings and dictators and envisioned a better world for themselves.

Unfortunately, being across the wide Atlantic Ocean did not totally remove them from the oppressive hand of King George III (Jun 4, 1738 – Jan 29, 1820), since America was considered to be a British possession, and he continued to demand more and more taxes. There was the Stamp Act and the Townshend Act (tea tax) which resulted in the Boston tea party on 16 Dec 1773.

King George was so desperate, or greedy, that he withheld money from the pay of his soldiers for food and lodging. Many of his soldiers who had been sent to the new world to fight the revolution came back sick or wounded. To pay for their needs he withheld a tax from the others, leaving many with as little as four pennies per day.

The men who set out to gain independence for the nation knew they were risking everything; life, property and freedom. Not everyone was in favor of such a move and were still considered to be loyalists in spite of feeling oppressed and overtaxed.

Decisions were not made quickly nor easily. It involved a lot of meetings and deliberations with a lot of disagreements but each one knew the importance of their task.

These men did not take their duties lightly. It took many years of thought and discussion but more taxation and control made many of them come to realize they could well do without Britain.

The reality of war opened the minds of many of the colonists when British soldiers were sent to Concord and Lexington in late 1775 to "bring them under control". The Second Continental Congress adopted the Declaration of Independence on July 2, 1776 and it was signed on July 4, by the 56 men who had originated it.

Their job was by no means done. Next came the Articles of Confederation in Nov 1777. The actual Constitution itself took many more years of discussion and fine-tuning and then the various amendments had to be decided, voted on and ratified.

Probably very few Americans are aware of the fate of these fifty-six brave men who risked so much.

Five signers were captured by the British as traitors and tortured before they died. Twelve had their homes ransacked and burned. Two lost their sons in the war: another had two sons captured. Nine of them fought and died of wounds or hardships of the war.

They signed and they pledged their lives, their fortunes and their sacred honor.

What kind of men were they?

Twenty-four were lawyers and jurists. Eleven were merchants and nine were farmers and plantation owners, men of means, well educated. But they signed the Declaration of Independence knowing full well that the penalty would be death if captured.

Carter Braxton of Virginia, a wealthy planter and trader, saw his ships swept from the seas by the British Navy. He sold his home and properties to pay his debts and died in rags.

Thomas McKeam was so hounded by the British the he was forced to move his family almost constantly. He served in Congress without pay, and his family was kept in hiding. His possessions were taken from him and poverty was his reward.

Vandals or soldiers looted the properties of Dillery, Hall, Clymer, Walton, Gwinnett, Heyward, Rutledge and Middleton.

At the battle of Yorktown, Thomas Nelson, Jr. noted that the British General Cornwallis had taken over the Nelson home for his headquarters. He quietly urged Gen. George Washington to open fire. The home was destroyed and Nelson died totally bankrupt.

Francis Lewis had his home and properties destroyed. The enemy jailed his wife and she died within a few months.

John Hart was driven from his wife's bedside as she was dying. Their thirteen children fled for their lives and his fields and gristmill were laid to waste. For more than a year, he lived in forests and caves, returning home to find his wife dead and his children vanished. A few weeks later he died from exhaustion and a broken heart.

Norris and Livingston suffered similar fates.

Such were the stories and sacrifices of the American Revolution. These were not wild-eyed, rabble-rousing ruffians. They were soft-spoken men of means and education. They had security but they valued liberty more.

Standing tall, straight and unwavering, they pledged: "For the support of this declaration, with firm reliance on the protection of the Devine Providence, we mutually pledge to each other our lives, our fortunes, and our sacred honor".

They gave you and me a free and independent America. The history books never told you a lot about what happened in the Revolutionary War. We didn't fight just the British. We were British subjects at the time, and we fought our own government as well.

Some of us take these liberties for granted but we shouldn't.

Author Unknown

Another one of the signers of the Declaration of Independence, with whom I am familiar, was Robert Morris of Pennsylvania, from the book *"Robert Morris, Audacious Patriot"* by Frederick Wagner. Published by Dodd Mead, NY.

Before the war Morris had risen from modest beginnings to being quite wealthy. He became a strong supporter of the American cause and close friends with George Washington and their families socialized often. At one point Morris bought a new home and Washington moved into the home that the Morris' moved out of.

Morris provided much of the financial support for the army of Gen. Washington and the new government. He spent pretty much his entire fortune in supporting the new nation, ended up broke and in debtors' prison for three years and six months. He died penniless on May 8, 1806 and was buried in Christ Churchyard in Philadelphia.

Although he had spent his entire fortune helping to bring about American Independence, people soon forgot. Strangely enough many people are just as forgetful today.

As history plainly shows, multitudes of people have made the ultimate sacrifice to keep us free. From Bunker Hill to San Juan Hill. From the trenches of France to the Sands of Iwo Jima and all the other Hell holes where Americans have fought and died and are still dying for the same reason. **No. Freedom is not free.**

"Freedom is never more than a single generation from extinction". Ronald Reagan

The efforts of many years of hard work and sacrifice resulted in what is perhaps the greatest document ever conceived by man, second only to the Holy Bible. No doubt because much of the Constitution is based on the ten commandments of God. Most of our founding fathers were men of God and, as they pledged in forming the Declaration of Independence, had a firm reliance on the protection of the Devine Providence.

I have often felt that our government would have fared much better through the years if our political leaders had kept the same attitude and based all decisions on only the Bible and the Constitution. Unfortunately, too many other influences have been allowed to creep into the daily operations. Today we have people working very hard to dispose of both the Bible and the Constitution. It's time to take a stand against the heathens of the world.

The Founding Fathers Were Kids!

Aaron Burr, was an officer in the Continental Army at age 20 and eventually served as the memorable third vice president of the United States

Alexander Hamilton, was 22 when appointed chief of staff to General George Washington. He became one of the most influential promoters of the Constitution and the founder of the first American political party.

James Madison, 25 was instrumental in the drafting of our Constitution and the writing of the Bill of Rights. He was the fourth U.S, president.

Marquis de LaFayette, was only 19 when he served as a major general in the Continental Army under George Washington.

James Monroe, 18, was a lieutenant in Washington's army. He became the fifth U.S. president and the last of the founding fathers to serve as president.

Readers Digest – March 2014

COLLAPSE OF SOCIETY

"The greatness of America lies in the character of our people...in simple virtues like faith, hard work, marriage, family, personal responsibility and helping the least of us"
Faith and Freedom Coalition – Feb 2020

Our founding fathers intended that government do two basic things: provide for the common defense of the nation, and to *promote* the general welfare. It was not intended to *provide* for the general welfare.

"If anyone will not work, let him not eat"
2 Thessalonians 3:10 RSV

For the first hundred years or so the people of the new nation were almost totally self-reliant. The family unit was the core of society with the father, as head of household, doing whatever was necessary to take care of his family. If a person suffered illness or injury, or other major disaster, his extended family and neighbors stepped up to get the family through the crisis. Anything from planting or harvesting the crops or the task of rebuilding a house or barn destroyed by fire or windstorm.

"Love thy neighbor as thy self".
Leviticus 19:18 KJV

Around the beginning of the twentieth century the whole world seemed to start changing drastically; with industrial growth, advancements in technology, and education. Even politics took on a whole new meaning.

Hardly more than a decade of the new century had passed when the world became involved in World War One (WWI). The War to end all wars. This was the first war to utilize mechanized vehicles, aircraft and even greater weapons to kill.

As though war was not killing enough people the world was hit by a pandemic of influenza in 1918 that killed an estimated fifty million people worldwide and approximately 675,000 in the United States. There were no flu vaccines at the time.

At the end of WWI the world was still in a state of depression but the people were happy to have it behind them and started celebrating. Good times were here again, It became known as the *Roaring Twenties*.

During the twenties people were so busy having fun and living it up they felt like they were on top of the world. The president of the New York Federal Reserve, created in 1913, later called the Governor of the Federal Reserve, a man by the name of Benjamin Strong, had ideas on keeping the economy afloat by means of bond-buying campaigns. This was to drive down interest rates relative to London. This encouraged the British creditors to keep their money in higher yielding Sterling rather than converting to gold or dollars.

Due to splendid tax cuts and budget surpluses, the American economy was flush with cash and the U. S. Banking system was quite liquid, creating a bubble. Coupled with low interest rates, below three percent, Strong's meddling in the money market caused the economy to tank. He became known as *Bubble Ben 1.0* thereafter.

Strong's ultra-low interest rates did cause credit growth but did not end up funding steel mills or auto plants. Instead, it flooded Wall Street's Call money market and fueled the greatest debt-driven stock market bubble in history. By 1929 the margin debt soared to 12% of GDP. The bubble also spawned a boom in foreign bonds. The Depression became a worldwide problem.

President Herbert Hoover was elected in late 1928 and took office in March 1929. A few months later the stock market crashed bringing about the Great Depression. Of course the opposition party quickly blamed him for the crash which had been coming for several years. To this day there are still people who believe the political propaganda that circulated. Many people lost their entire life's savings and investments. Thousands of people were put out of work and most banks closed. The Federal Deposit Insurance Corporation (FDIC) did not exist in those times.

"I want to say that despite our troubles and the implacable enemies in many parts of the world who threaten our way of life, we will come through. We will

come through because we have the best form of government and productive genius, because we have freedom and courage to protect it and, above all, because we believe in God. That last is a priceless advantage that our atheistic enemies don't have".

President Herbert Hoover in the dark days of the depression.

President Franklin D. Roosevelt took office in 1933 and, like most new presidents, started trying to put his own ideas into practice. The world was in desperate shape and something had to be done.

One of his first efforts was made in 1933, shortly after his inauguration. At the time most of the world's finances were based on a thing called *the gold standard,* which, theoretically, held government overspending and inflation in check. Roosevelt apparently found this to be a little too restrictive and had the rule demolished. This gave government the option of cranking up the trusty printing presses and cranking out car-loads of our paper money. Greenbacks. Legal counterfeiting. Needless to say, the monster called inflation came very much alive.

In order to put people back to work Roosevelt initiated a couple of government work programs. One was called CCC, meaning "Civilian Conservation Corps". The other was the WPA for "Work Projects Administration". To have employment for so many out-of-work people, a lot of menial jobs were created, such as manual labor on roads and highways. Anything from picking up trash to digging ditches. The pay was quite low but people were desperate. Even though most of the men were happy to be working, apparently some took advantage of the lack of supervision and goofed off about as much as they worked. Some joked about it and said WPA stood for "we piddle around". In those days *piddle* was a word for *tinker* or non-serious effort.

The FDIC (Federal Deposit Insurance Corp) was the Glass-Steagall Act of 1933 and was based on the Deposit Insurance enacted in Massachusetts.

In 1935 FDR came up with his plan known as *"The New Deal"* to give financial aid to the aged, infirmed and the unemployed, which was to ensure that economic, social and political benefits of *American Capitalism* were distributed more "equally" among America's large and diverse populace. Obviously without requiring any effort or work on the part of that *diverse* populace. Sounds very much like Socialism. Some took that to mean a life-long gravy train.

No doubt Roosevelt's giveaway programs became the answer to many prayers and convinced a large part of the "populace" that the government was their savior who would take care of their every need. This brought about his being elected for a third term. Apparently it also made many politicians aware that votes could be bought with massive giveaways funded by tax dollars. It has gotten worse with each passing year.

During the years of the Great Depression which affected the entire world, Adolph Hitler convinced the people of Germany that he could solve all their problems if he was made chancellor.

He started gathering about him a lot of the street rabble, hoodlums, put brown shirts on them and called them his storm troopers. Through threats, intimidation and outright violence he was able to coerce the nation's officials to grant his every wish. (Much like today). Due to the Nazis' violence and growing civil unrest, Chancellor Paul Von Hindenburg appointed Hitler as chancellor on Jan 30, 1933. Hitler then declared himself dictator of the Third Reich in 1935.

Any nation that might offer resistance he signed non-aggression pacts with their leaders, including Britain's Prime Minister Neville Chamberlain, who then returned to England bragging about his "appeasement policy" with Hitler. He was convinced war had been averted. Within days, or weeks, Hitler's armies would move into these countries and take them over. The smaller countries were just attacked without warning.

Italy's Benito Mussolini, "Il Duce", then joined forces with Hitler in 1940. Many Italian people were not in favor of such a partnership but Mussolini was also a dictator. It was said that a lot of the Italian soldiers very quickly surrendered when they got into battle because they were against it.

Hirohito was emperor of Japan from 1926 to 1989. There were some who believed that he was not in favor of World War II but Tojo Hideki became dictator in 1941 leaving Hirohito as emperor and convincing his armies and navies that they were fighting for the honor of the Emperor.

Many Americans felt that the war going on in Europe did not concern us and insisted that we not get involved. But on Dec. 7, 1941 Japan attacked Pearl Harbor, Hawaii killing hundreds of our servicemen and women as well as civilians. This changed the minds of most Americans and the military recruiting offices of every branch of service were jammed with volunteers.

These three monsters, disciples of Satan, Hitler, Mussolini and Tojo became partners in the scheme to take over the world by force. Their alliance became known as the Axis. We can but wonder which of the three thought he would be top-dog if they were actually successful in conquering the world. More than likely each one thought *he* would rule. I'm sure we can all thank God and thousands of very brave men and women around the globe who fought, and many died, to prevent such a disaster from taking place. Thanks to their many sacrifices, we are still free. ***"No. Freedom is not free."***

With America being a quiet, peace-loving nation the people had, perhaps become complacent and even naïve. We were not really prepared for war and were caught completely off-guard when the Japanese attacked Pearl Harbor. Many of our naval vessels and aircraft were destroyed or badly damaged.

However, being a nation of resilience, ingenuity and determination, as well as short fuses, this all changed very quickly. Production plants started turning out needed war materials on a twenty-four-hour basis. People immediately volunteered for any job that would make a difference in the war effort. We were mad and wanted to show it. Housewives became factory workers, "Rosie the Riveters", and people started growing Victory gardens in their back yards. Many of Hollywood's most famous movie stars volunteered for military service or helping in war-bond drives, USO clubs, or entertaining the troops.

There was a totally different mentality and attitude at that time. Perhaps that is why the people who heled to win WWII have been called "The Greatest Generation".

U.S. Marines raising the American Flag on Mount Suribachi, Iwo Jima, February 23, 1945.

"This is the land of the Free, because of the Brave".

GOVERNMENT

"Government is not the solution to our problem, government is the problem". Ronald Reagan

Amendment X: "The powers not delegated to the United States by the Constitution, nor prohibited by it to the States, are reserved to the States respectively, or to the people."

The U.S. Constitution was written by wise, caring men, with much thought and deliberation, as a combination guide book and rule book. It served as a road map, or blue-print, for forming our government based on the knowledge and wisdom of these men as to the nature of people who are allowed positions of power. It was written to protect the rights and freedoms of each individual.

George Washington became our first president in 1789 and took office on Wall Street in New York. When re-elected in 1792 the capital had moved to Philadelphia, Pa where it remained for almost a decade.

Washington was a devout Christian with total faith in God. He was known to pray throughout the day and felt that he was protected by the Providence of God. On an occasion while fighting in the French and Indian war, for three hours he was exposed to the aim of expert marksmen; two horses fell from under him and a third was wounded. Four musket balls pierced his coat, and several grazed his sword. Every other officer was killed or wounded, and only he remained unhurt. The Indians directed their arrows towards his breast, and the French made him a target   for their rifles, but both were harmless. His safety astonished his savage enemies, and they called him "The Spirit-protected man, who would be a chief of nations."

But, even he had detractors. Several, unsigned letters were sent to various members of congress during the war years, accusing him of wrongdoings and urging his removal as commander of the Armies. *(Sounds very much like the anonymous whistleblowers of today).* Even though he had the utmost confidence and support of his men and every member of congress there were still enemies. Washington encouraged Congress to fully investigate the matter.

Even as a schoolboy he had a strong reputation for honesty and integrity. It was said that his classmates would ask him to arbitrate and rule on their childish disagreements, knowing he would be fair and impartial.

In his farewell address, Washington warned the people against political parties, stating they would divide the nation and would lead to one group gaining the upper hand which could bring about a dictatorial government.

The original Capitol building was completed in 1800 and served as the home of Congress and the legislative branch. The building was badly burned in 1814, by the

British, in the war of 1812 but was fully restored within five years. A dome was added in 1818.

The building was doubled in size in 1850 and the dome replaced with the current design, three times the height of the original. The "Statue of Freedom" was installed on top of the dome in 1863 with the motto "Triumphant in War and Peace".

The first president to be inaugurated in the new Capitol was Thomas Jefferson, in March 1801. Even though the new government was less than two decades old, partisan politics and maneuverings had already begun. Jefferson had received slightly more than sixty-five percent of the popular vote but his confirmation was held up by one vote and that one man was leaning toward Jefferson's opponent.

Well, the people still had vivid memories of the Revolutionary war, in which many had taken part. Most had lost loved ones as well. Not willing to allow the freedoms they had fought for to be trampled by politics, a large number of them marched into DC with muskets and pitchforks. The one last individual was confronted and *persuaded* to vote with the majority. Jefferson became the third president.

As Washington predicted, political parties have definitely divided our nation. Perhaps in the beginning they merely had different ideologies on government but obviously too many radicals have become involved and wish to convert us to socialism, or worse.

As previously stated, our founding fathers knew human nature and the evil found within the hearts of many. If one reads Ancient History, greed and the lust for power go back to the beginning of time. To acquire the throne or position of power, men would kill their brother, or even their father, to gain such power. Royal children have been killed by those competing for the throne.

Today's politicians are no less hungry for the rewards that high office can offer. There have been many rumors in our own time of political enemies who have met with untimely death, under suspicious circumstances; eg, accident, suicide, or heart attacks in people who were known to be quite healthy.

Career politicians have become quite adept at convincing people that they have all the answers. When in pursuit of office they tell the people what they are going to do *for* us. Once in office it becomes what they are going to do *to* us. It seems the proclamation of "government of the people, by the people, for the people" as Lincoln put it in his Gettysburg Address, has become a thing of the past.

No doubt many young politicians go into office with ideas of doing great things and making a difference. But once among the lions with experience, they find that they can accomplish nothing unless they are willing to go along with selfish schemes of the entrenched. Very much like a young criminal who goes to prison and learns the ropes from the hardened criminals, In my opinion, many politicians are just street criminals who were lucky enough to get an education. Without such an education a lot of them would be on the streets committing crimes instead of legal fraud in office.

"Power corrupts; absolute power corrupts absolutely."

Do I sound bitter? You bet your patootie I am. I detest people trying to destroy the greatest nation on God's green earth. Are we perfect? Of course not. We are still human, but I think most people try.

As the saying goes, "people deserve the kind of government they vote for". This is brought about by the fact that many people are too lazy to research the issues, or question how the person stands that they're voting for. They vote for the person that's *good looking*, or sounds nice. Or they believe the wild promises that common sense should tell them he can't accomplish. Of course the promise of lots of freebies goes a long way.

Also, many people vote for an individual and once he is in office they never contact him, or her, and don't bother to find out how that person is voting on critical matters. One of my brothers had a friend who was elected to a state office and he told my brother that he was amazed that he never heard a word from any of his constituents.

A friend of mine was elected to the state legislature. He said that before being elected he wondered why it took so long to get anything accomplished. After he got into those hallowed halls he was amazed that anything was *ever* accomplished.

Many politicians tend to use only those parts of the Constitution that aid or justify their schemes. All other parts they try to change or just ignore.

Our enemies have succeeded in infiltrating our government. I believe it was Vladimir Lenin who made a long list of things they could do to destroy our government as we know it. His list included things like "destroy the Church (Christianity), get the young people interested in alcohol, sex and drugs, dilute the laws and infiltrate the politics. Disarm the police". It appears they have accomplished most of these plans.

It amazes me that so many people come to America, supposedly because they were unhappy with the conditions in their home countries, and yet, they get here and start taking part in protests against the way things are done here or against our form of government. If they want the type of government from which they fled, the answer is simple. Just go back there.

Perhaps some of them come here, with a lot of patience, with the idea of getting the right to vote, or maybe having their children become involved in our political system, in order to change this to the type of government they knew before.

An example is one Rashida Tlaib, D-Mi a member of Congress. I had the great displeasure of watching a video of her speaking to a group of people who, judging from their reactions, were in full agreement with her.

She stated *"our final objective is not just to become part of the system, but to create our own Muslim system, to look at all the other people who are sharing this country with us as potential Muslims.* (Notice, she did not say "all the other people with whom we are sharing this country". She said *"all the other people who are sharing this country with **us**").* She went on to say *"We have an obligation to try to bring them into the same style of thinking, same way of behaving".*

She continued with *"we have a long-range process of making America Muslim. **All** of America Muslim. We must have some short-range goals. We have to be very **calculated*** *about it or we will not accomplish our goals".* I wonder, do these goals include beheading us? (Emphasis added).

My question is, has she ever sworn an allegiance to our flag or to America? Has she sworn to uphold and protect the Constitution? **Wake up America.**

And then we have Alexandria Ocasio-Cortez, D-NY. (Democratic Socialists of America). How obvious is that?

Sadly, it's not just people of foreign extraction who are trying to destroy our nation and our way of life. We have the left-leaning politicians and those who freely admit their Socialist ideals. Most are natural-born citizens who call themselves "progressives" and consider themselves to be the *elite*. These are individuals who have been blest with great wealth or have found ways to lie, cheat and steal their way to the top. The Swamp.

One would think they would have some gratitude or even a degree of fondness for the country that allowed them the opportunity to gain such assets and political power. But, it seems they only think of the people as naïve fools to be taken advantage of.

Consider the Clintons who left the White House claiming they were broke and actually asked for donations to help pay some of Bill's expenses in his impeachment trial. Today they are millionaires.

We also have people like Bernie Sanders, an admitted lover of Socialism. Joe Biden who doesn't really call himself a Socialist but expresses all the traits, and plans, of such. Andrew Cuomo who seems to be cut from the same cloth. These people all promise a world of free everything. Free healthcare for ALL (Socialized medicine). Free education and guaranteed income for all. They don't say how all this will be paid for.

And, perhaps the worst of the lot, and the most dangerous of them all, is George Sorros, a Hungarian-born socialist who has vowed to "bring this nation to it's knees".

Sorros has an estimated worth of something in the neighborhood of twenty-seven BILLION dollars, which he is spending like a drunken sailor, to destroy the country. He owns, or controls by donations, almost every major news outlet in America. Including a donation of more than a million dollars to National Public Radio. No wonder we have fake news. Sadly, too many people are easily bought, by paychecks as employees, or through outright bribes and promises of freebies.

It's a puzzle to me why he cannot be charged with espionage, sedition, or even *hymopery*. Anything to put a stop to his destructive intentions. One would think there would be enough people who take his money, that would realize what he plans for us, and refuse to believe any of his left-wing garbage. The money is not worth helping him flush the nation down the toilet.

Unfortunately, the term "sheeple" has come to be an accurate description of too many. The magic word "free" is all some can think about and are willing to sell their rights, liberties and souls for temporary benefits. They are blinded by the word "free", and are buying into Globalism; one-world government. And many of these "sheeple" consider themselves patriotic, Christian Americans. Just don't take away their cold beer and TV remote. Their chains are being forged as we speak.

"A nation of sheep breeds a government of wolves".

THE LOSS OF OUR CONSTITUTION

"Peace is that brief glorious moment in
history, when everybody stands around reloading"

Thomas Jefferson

The magnificent document known world-wide as the US
Constitution was written for the protection and benefit of
the people and our nation as a whole, not as a means for
the career politicians to enslave and control the people. It
was meant to provide freedom and liberty unknown by
other nations. *Term limits, maybe?*

Unfortunately, through the years, politicians have
evolved into controllers and not leaders. Their objective
is to manipulate and control our every move while trying
to convince us they are doing what's best for us. That's
why they are making a concerted effort to totally destroy
our Constitution. The number one target of the left-wing
liberals (Socialists), is the 2nd Amendment.

If they can eradicate the 2nd Amendment, the First
Amendment will be next. After that the remainder of

the Constitution will be of no value. The authors of the Constitution put in the 2nd Amendment to protect us from the very kind of people who are trying so hard to destroy it.

They try to convince people that taking guns away from the honest, law-abiding citizens will stop the murders and assaults; perhaps all crime.

Well, nothing could be further from the truth. In my years in law-enforcement I saw people killed, injured and maimed by all sorts of weapons – no guns involved. Some of these assaults were committed with vehicles, caustic chemicals, knives, chains, dynamite and plain old broomsticks or clubs.

Even cavemen killed each other and guns had never been heard of. When an individual makes up his mind to kill or be destructive, he will find a way. But if guns are taken away from law-abiding souls in today's world, they will be at the mercy of every type of criminal, including politicians, with no way to defend themselves or their families. As the saying goes, *"when guns are outlawed, only outlaws will have guns"*. But, perhaps if I treated, or mistreated, the people the way the politicians do, maybe I wouldn't want them to have guns either.

In 2013 New York state passed a law called *"We ask everyone – Firearm safety is a health issue"*. This law, eagerly signed by Andrew Cuomo, requires doctors, emergency room personnel and mental health workers to question patients about firearm ownership or guns in their homes. (NRA – Dec. 2020).

This information is then passed on to the NY State Division of Criminal Justice. This questioning is required of all patients entering the ER, even for auto accident injuries or Covid-19. Firearm safety is not the issue. The criminal nut-cases are the issue. Sadly, too many health care workers will abide by such a stupid law. Without regards to the rights of citizens.

This is just another example of how many of our left-wing politicians are using any means at their disposal to take ALL guns out of the hands of law-abiding people while releasing violent criminals back onto our streets. These same politicians will tell you they are all for "law and order and public safety", while in reality they want us to have no means of defense.

This points out, quite clearly, why people need to pay attention to what their elected officials stand for. To put them into office based on their glowing promises and then leave them to pursue their own agenda is a classic case of putting the fox in the chicken house.

Just turning such people loose in our government, without demanding they do what we elected them to do, is how DC has become a *swamp*.

Many of these people are elected by ner-do-well deadbeats and people who have been totally brainwashed. The magic word *free* buys a lot of votes. It's time for more True Americans to play a role in the selection of people entrusted with the future of our great Nation. Voting is a Constitutional right but I sometimes wonder if there should be some kind of qualifying test. At least nineteen states have re-call provisions for many of their elected officials. Sounds like a good idea.

In 1940, at the beginning of WWII, the British evacuated some 338,000 of their troops from Dunkirk but had to leave 40,000 soldiers behind who became prisoners of the Nazis. Many did not survive.

Prime Minister Winston Churchill asked for 500,000 volunteers for a militia. But, instead he got three times as many as he asked for.

The nation was not prepared for war because, like America, and most peace-loving people, they were naïve' enough to believe all people felt the same. And to make it worse they also had government officials who did not believe the people needed to be armed.

The British Government was faced with the task of preparing for war, along with re-supplying and equipping many of the men rescued from Dunkirk and finding enough arms to equip over a million volunteers. Many of them started the war with only their personal hunting rifles and shotguns. Britain had made the mistake of "firearms regulation" in 1920 and 1937, that effectively disarmed the citizens.

This should serve as a vivid lesson to us today what our founding fathers meant in the Second Amendment about a "well-armed" militia being necessary for the security of a free State. The Constitution belongs to the people. Not the politicians.

There is little doubt (by most true Americans) that our Nation has avoided invasion by enemy troops for the past two-hundred years because so many of our citizens are armed and prepared to use their weapons in defense of our country. Of course there have been those who have sneaked in under pretense of being friends of visitors, to infiltrate....to commit acts of sedition and espionage. But the largest number of these "sneak-thieves" have been the socialists and its time they are recognized for what they are …the enemy, and repulsed.

The left-wing radicals tell us that the confiscation of all guns will stop the nut-cases and disciples of Satan from doing harm. They say that law-abiding people don't need guns for protection; that we have police officers to protect us. As a former police officer, I can tell you that law-enforcement cannot be everywhere at once. Especially in today's psychopathic world.

The crux of the 2nd Amendment states quite explicitly: *"The right of the people to keep and bear arms, **shall not be infringed**"*. It does not say "only if approved by George Sorros, Mike Bloomburg, Elizabeth Warren, Joe Biden, Nancy Pislosi or other left-wing socialist. They try very hard to disarm us while they have well-armed security people all around them.

"Men who hammer their guns into plow shears will plow for those who do not". Thomas Jefferson

Anyone who says taking guns out of the hands of any law-abiding citizens will stop the killings or the mass-shootings is either a fool, a liar, or both.

It's understandable that people who have lost loved ones to these nut-cases can be convinced that gun-control, now called gun-safety, will prevent another one. It's easy for them to believe the propaganda spewing from these radicals pretending to be concerned about the loss of their loved one, when their only concern is making sure the American people have no defense against their dictatorial laws and actions

Perhaps I am naïve but it's impossible for me to understand how people can reap such great rewards, advantages and freedoms from this country and still want, so desperately, to destroy it. Maybe I should say their *ill-gotten* wealth. That's *ill* as in illegal, illegitimate and mentally ill. No doubt all these terms apply to the retarded socialists.

They want open borders (no borders). Free every-thing for the illegals, guaranteed income for the lazy deadbeats and an enormous tax system that will make it even more difficult for the working people. Knowing quite well, the deadbeats are not going to vote against Santa Claus. How can any reasonably sane person, who cares a hoot about this country, allow themselves to be stupefied by such socialist rhetoric. No doubt it's the years of brainwashing by the media and our schools.

So many Americans have become much too unconcerned or lazy, or perhaps they think the problems will resolve themselves. The "ostrich syndrome". The problems will be resolved when our nation is under the control of the Socialists or the Muslims, but, then it's too late to think about it. They need to realize, the enemy within, both foreign and domestic, never rests. They have programs in place that work twenty-four hours a day and those programs are paid for and directed by the George Sorros', the Andrew Cuomo's and the Bernie Sanders' of the world. Those who have the most American dollars. They plan to use American money and the U.S. Constitution to enslave us. Unfortunately, the Sheeple don't seem concerned.

It's too bad the people didn't listen to the advice of George Washington and stay away from political parties. Each individual should run for office based solely on his own merits, without party affiliation.   Therehave been many times I have heard the claim, or excuse, "my granddaddy was a democrat, my daddy was a democrat and I'm a democrat". Some even say "I don't like that candidate but I'm a democrat so I have to vote for him". Duh? Like one lady in my brother's church. She promised her father, more than forty years ago, that she would always vote democrat.

The ignorance, or lack of concern, has allowed the "elite" to create a totally regulatory state that governs our every action, and to an extent, our every thought. A condition almost impossible to reverse.

My concern, my main question is, if the Socialists get total control, how many military leaders and law enforcement officials will refuse to go along with their destruction of our Constitution? If Any. Or will they just roll over and play dead?

*"Our Constitution was made only for **moral** and **religious** people. It is wholly inadequate to the government of any other."*

John Adams
America's second President

TAXES AND REVENUE

Taxpayer: "Someone who works for the Federal government but doesn't have to take a civil service exam"
Ronald Reagan

The U.S. Constitution, (Sect. 7, 8, & 9) allows for taxation. The sixteenth amendment allowed for the start of an income tax, Feb. 1913, possibly not ratified, it is believed that it was done to cover the expense of WWI. One train of thought is that the framers of our Constitution meant only property taxes, excise taxes and import/export taxes. Too bad they didn't give a little more thought to the greed of future politicians and put a limit on the number of things which can be taxed.

At the start of the twentieth century, there were so few taxes you could count them on one hand, and this was the most prosperous nation on earth and we had no national debt. Today, a hundred years later, there are so many taxes it would take hours, if not days, to list them all. As best I can ascertain, there are close to two hundred various taxes and the list is growing.

We had no sales tax until the states of Kentucky and Mississippi started them in 1930, perhaps because of the great depression. Kentucky repealed theirs in 1936 but it didn't take long for officials of **all** states to realize this was too good to pass up. In the past thirty years I have seen *temporary* increases in sales tax for such things as street or highway maintenance or to "bail out the schools". Obviously *temporary* means until they can think of an excuse to raise them again.

Great Britain is well known for taxation and they are believed to have started the first income tax to wage war with Napoleon.

We now have more taxes than fleas on a whole pack of stray dogs. Besides the usual income tax, sales tax and property tax, we have taxes on services, such as home and auto repairs, parts and labor, even on mail-order items. Section nine of the Constitution states *"no tax or duty shall be laid on articles exported from any state"*. Does this not make such a tax unconstitutional?

Some states even charge the people an *annual* tax on appliances and other household goods, even though they paid sales tax at the time of purchase. Talk about double taxation. The bite is even greater on people who decide to go into business.

Even our telephone and utility services have become a great source of tax revenue. In most locals today, you must have internet service to have a regular home phone. No land wire phones.

They start with a Satellite programming tax, then an administrative charge, a Federal universal service charge, regulatory cost-recovery charge (whatever that is). Next comes County interstate sales tax, county telecom fee, state 911 service fee, and that's okay, and a state telecom tax.

The utility company then hits us with similar costs. There is a "gas adjustment charge" on natural gas; a "fuel cost adjustment on electricity" The tax on our water is the same as buying merchandise at the store. This is topped with a "sewer charge" which is based on the amount of water we use. And, if that's not enough, there is a county mosquito and rodent-control fee and a city storm water fee. The list goes on and on.

Today's politicians would make King George III proud, even envious, with their many laws and taxes, the likes of which he never dreamed.

Auto tags have become another burden, and then they add on gas tax and wheel tax, No doubt many cities and states still have auto inspections which they say is to increase vehicle safety. Perhaps, but my guess is, it's for the revenue collected.

Auto inspections were started locally in 1934, and the price was fifty cents per inspection, three times a year. That was still the price in the nineteen-fifties. By the time it was discontinued in June of 2013 the price was twenty-five dollars, or so, per year. The cost had been rolled into the auto-tag renewal and was shown as one price but when inspections were discontinued the cost was not. Enough is never enough.

Most working people must have a car to get to work, get to doctors' appointments and get the kids to soccer practice and to school. The family car has become pretty much a necessity, but has also become a great source of revenue for government. When you buy a car, there is sales tax, title fees and tags. If you decide a short time later, or anytime, the car is not what you need and sell it, that person has to pay all the same costs on that car and if you buy another car you start all over again. This could happen if a car is sold once a week.

Throughout our entire working life we are paying income tax, social security tax and medicare tax, and yet the liberal politicians talk about privatizing our Social Security and medicare or doing away with them all together. They often refer to them as "entitlement" programs like they are just government "handouts" even though we have paid into them our entire life. But strangely enough, you never hear any mention of cutting back or doing away with welfare and food stamps, or ADC for people who never seek employment. It's called "buying the vote".

The Social Security Act was signed into law on August 14, 1935 by FDR, along with welfare and other "social insurance" programs. It was originally called the "Economic Security" bill but the name was changed to SSA during consideration by Congress. Medicare was signed into law on July 30, 1965 but beneficiaries were first able to sign up for it on July 1, 1966.

Under the original law passed in 1935 social security only paid retirement benefits for the "primary" worker. In 1939 an amendment added survivors' benefits for spouse and children. Disability benefits were added in 1956. The original 1935 law included the first national unemployment compensation program, aid to states for health programs, and ADC benefits.

For many years now there have been reports that the

S/S fund has been raided by DC bureaucrats (swamp rats) and replaced with a lot of IOU's.

If you research the subject, the Google report states this is a *"misunderstanding"* or *"confusion"* between the financing of the S/S program and the way the S/S trust fund is treated in the Federal budget accounting. (Sounds like smoke and mirrors to me).

Due to actions by the Johnson Administration, in 1968. the Budget Accounting transactions of the Trust Fund were included in what was called the "unified budget". This meant every function of the U.S. government is included in a single budget. This continued until 1990 when the Trust Funds were again taken "off-budget", which means only that they are shown as separate accounts. Again, smoke and mirrors but no indication that any of the IOU's were ever repaid to the S/S fund.

It appears to me that most laws passed today are to create more revenue, more control and, perhaps, to protect the criminal element instead of the law-abiding citizen. The victim. Of course most legislators have, for many years, had a liberal attitude towards making laws that generate revenue.

Traffic laws seem to be the most lucrative with officers being made to write tickets even at the expense of a higher crime rate. Most departments today give the officers a quota they must reach. They are not allowed to show any tolerance because the officials want the revenue. The department in which I worked did not have quotas and we were allowed to use our own discretion as to whether to write a ticket or just give a warning. We were never once told, when leaving role-call, "go write tickets". We were told "go fight crime".

Today there are traffic cameras, and there is a requirement to wear seatbelts. I firmly believe in seat belts but I think it's unconstitutional for the government to tell a grownup individual he *must* wear a seatbelt or pay a fine. *Revenue.* If still working as a police officer, I would not enforce it... (and lose my job no doubt).

CRIME AND THE CRIMINAL JUSTICE SYSTEM

When most politicians speak of stopping crime they immediately start talking about *gun control*, now called *gun safety*. They pretend to think that taking guns away from law-abiding citizens will cause the criminal to change his ways and become a decent person. I'm sure they know better.

It's true, many crimes are committed with guns, but the liberal courts find no problem releasing the bad guys back onto the street, time-and-time-again. It has gotten to the point that a person who gets a ticket for speeding, on his way to work, will end up paying more than the career criminal who gets arrested for burglary or armed robbery. Of course if he has a job he can add to the cities revenue while the career criminal is just an expense.

An arrest starts with a large amount of paperwork. Then he has to be transported to jail where he has to be processed (booked), fed and kept comfortable while awaiting trial. In most cases he can't afford a defense lawyer so he is furnished with a public defender. All at the public's expense. Needless to say, he is not charged a court cost as the working stiff is if he pleads "not guilty" on his speeding ticket.

Many a time I have heard officers complain that the criminal is back on the street before the paperwork is finished. Criminals know this, and some have even said so when arrested, so they don't worry about it.

The individual arrested for the murder of the NBA star, Lorenzen Wright, and still awaiting trial, was charged, along with Wright's wife who pled guilty to complicity in the matter. The judge hearing the preliminaries commented that the man charged had been arrested for seven different felonies and a gun was involved in at least five of the cases. Are we to believe he would not have done these crimes if only guns could be taken away from law-abiding people?

Sally Snowden McKay was stabbed to death (no gun) in her home on Horseshoe Lake in Eastern Arkansas in 1996 along with her nephew, Lee Baker, a popular Memphis blues/rock guitarist.

The suspects' family had lived on the victim's land for years and he entered a guilty plea to both murders. Ironically, the family of the victims, being Christian people, asked the court not to impose the death penalty. Instead of a life sentence, he was sentenced to twenty-five years and a few months. He was paroled in 2018.

The suspect, Travis Santay Lewis, returned to the area and on March 25, 2020 he killed the daughter of the woman he had murdered in 1996. This victim was Martha McKay, a 40-year-old. She was murdered in her home, a

B&B business she operated at the same lake. Lewis jumped into the lake to avoid capture by the police and drowned. Finally, justice was served.

There have been many, many cases where people have been convicted of brutal crimes and are given very light sentences, or had their sentence drastically reduced, and they commit an even worse crime within a very short time. If they were required to stay the course there would be far less crime, even without taking the guns of innocent citizens. As the saying goes, "if you do the crime, you do the time".

If you get the idea that many judges are too lenient, you might consider this; it seems that the bigger percentage of judges, for some reason, are former defense attorneys. They spend years working the system, looking for any loophole to get a sleazebag off. Suddenly he puts on the black robe and sits on the other side of the bench. What does he look for? Any little loophole or excuse to let the sleazebag off.

In my opinion, our crime rate is out of sight because the criminals are not treated like criminals. They are given special treatment. Lots of sympathy. All kinds of excuses are made for them. They grew up in poverty, broken homes, little education and no economic opportunities. They have learned how to milk the golden goose for all it's worth.

If growing up in poverty was an excuse, no doubt a lot of us would have ended up in jail. By today's standards, most everyone I knew while growing up was poor but we didn't know it. Times were hard and the work was hard.

We wore patches on our clothes but we had the main asset. A loving family and family pride.

Obviously family has a lot to do with how an individual turns out. If a child has a stable, loving family to take an interest in what he does, and teach him to have some pride and self-respect it will make a huge difference, no doubt. But, unfortunately, many parents of today grew up in a home, or homes, where they were taught nothing but bad habits. They, in turn, have children of their own and neglect or ignore them. Just leave it to the state. The problem just gets worse with time. Too bad there is not a rule, or regulation, for being a parent, Some way to hold them accountable. Come to think of it, there is, but it's God's rule and too many parents today don't have the time to apply His rules.

Unfortunately, too many of our, so-called, leaders in government don't want us to discipline our children. They want to control us and brainwash the children. *See the Communist manifesto.* So many times we hear of a parent being arrested just for spanking their child. *"Spare the rod, spoil the child".* No doubt my father would have been in trouble often.

Obviously kids need protecting from some of the parents of today. The alcoholics, the drug abusers and the ones who are just plain mean. Too bad there is not a test, or qualifying exam, that can be given before some are allowed to have a child. Of course that would be unconstitutional, but taking guns away from law-abiding people is not. (According to the Socialists).

Another crime which has become quite prevalent in today's world is "internet crime". People are being victimized by cyber thieves and hackers who seem to suffer no consequences.

It's amazing how crooks can "hack" into other accounts at random but government technology experts can't find e-mail information on the bad guys and prosecute them. Perhaps it's not considered a priority.

Dr. Phil has had several shows where he features people who were scammed out of thousands of dollars, and he would have investigators find these bums, usually someplace in South America, and actually confront them. The weird thing about it, the scammers seemed so unconcerned about being found. They seemed to look at the whole thing as just a way to make a living. A job. Our government needs to make the same effort to find these characters and take appropriate action. Perhaps it would be a good job for the old-time *Jersey Boys*.

The computer age came about as a means to make life easier, to enhance business and save time. Like so many things developed for the betterment of mankind, it fell into the hands of the crook with a devious, dishonest nature.

Today's hackers, scammers and crooks have become so sophisticated they can call you and have any number they wish show up on your caller ID. Even your own number. They can use face-book and display any face or picture, including a melding of various features from several people, to create a totally fictitious person. It's too bad some of them don't put their knowledge and talents to good use.

Another scam which has become much too common is to call people pretending to be from the IRS, or the local utility company. They tell the person they owe money for taxes or their utilities will be turned off at noon today if they don't run out, buy gift cards and call back with the appropriate numbers. Sometime the ruse is that they are calling from a law-enforcement agency and there is an outstanding warrant for a traffic citation and if they don't get those gift cards they will be arrested or be faced with other legal action.

Many people, especially the elderly, are gullible enough to believe them. Most people are law-abiding and don't want to become entangled in any kind of legal matter and will fall for the scam.

There have been numerous warnings about these scams and yet some believe they are in danger of legal action. They have been told that IRS does not call about delinquent taxes. The utility company does not call regarding late payments. These organizations send you a notice by U. S. Mail.

To me, every effort should be made to track down these scumbags, even in another country. Jail time is too good for them.

Another great danger of cyber-attack is the threat to the nation's power grids, a very real possibility. Current experience with the pandemic of Coronavirus illustrates the degree of panic that can occur amongst the people and this is small compared to loss of power on a large scale.

Such a power loss would close the banks, the gas stations and grocery stores immediately. Pretty much any type of operation, including hospitals, where people are so dependent on electrical power. No lights, nor heating and

AC. No refrigeration, so many foods would spoil in a very short time. We are not prepared for it.

People become involved with the police or with paramedics, by committing crimes or other stupid acts. Quite often they end up being injured or perhaps even being killed. Almost immediately the family and friends start making excuses for them and demanding that the *officers* be punished. The well-known rabble rousers, and some politicians, are ready to join in and criticize, even before all the facts are in. They insist that police get all the facts and be sure of the person's guilt *before* doing anything, and maybe that's as it should be, but a crime cannot be investigated from across town.

Our enemies insist that we play by the rules (the Constitution) but they never do. I have known of cases being thrown out of court because of a misspelled word.

Yes, the law-abiding people must play by the rules while being attacked from all sides. Not only by the street criminals but being drained of all resources and means of protection by many of the elected officials. It's like one of my friends said' "The first rule in a gun-fight is to have a gun".

Criminals will be criminals and we need to realize the fact. Almost from the beginning now there have been radical politicians and bleeding hearts who claim that light jail sentences, or no jail time, will reform them. But, the time for love and kindness is when the child is small. If they are taught love, respect and personal responsibility while growing up, these qualities will normally become a way of life. Of course these teachings must be done along with the appropriate amount of discipline. They learn that touching a hot stove can be painful.

Far too many people have come to disrespect our police officers. Some have a fierce hatred for them. Are police officers perfect? Of course not. They are people who can feel joy, or anger, or lose their patience when they see violence, or an individual mistreating another.

Most people who go into law-enforcement do so with a strong desire to fulfill the officer's motto *"to protect and serve"*. Their hope is to make a difference. To do good for those who need help. Unfortunately, they see the bad side of society so much that they sometimes start believing that everyone is bad.

Perhaps the two most important aspects of hiring a police officer are, a thorough and complete background investigation. Check on his character, personality, and attitudes (including any criminal record) by contacting people who have known him through the years. The next step is a thorough training program. These cannot be stressed strongly enough.

The department where I spent my years had very stringent requirements. Their qualifying standards were the same as for entry into West Point, except the usual recommendation of your congressman was not required. At that time, they were hiring one out of a hundred and the training never stopped. The first thing we were issued, before the badge, uniform or weapon, was a copy of the Constitution. No doubt most departments today would find these things too expensive, but the results are well worth the cost.

However, even the best officers can become tired and

frustrated by those in our society who want to destroy them, Are there officers who should not be officers? Yes. Officers need better training as do many people.

People have been brainwashed and manipulated, by the enemy within, to believe that all police officers are bad causing them to fear and hate the ones who are there to protect us. Which has, no doubt, caused some police officers to feel this hatred and become frustrated and to lose their patience. As previously stated, police officers are also human.

Needless to say, such a relationship is not always the best. But, for those of us who have been around for a long time, things were far worse in the past.

There was a time when the only requirement to be a police officer was the willingness to pin on a badge, strap on a weapon and go out and put one's life in danger. There was little requirement for education, knowledge of human nature, or even a great deal of honesty. Of course the pay was very small and ways to supplement it were built into the system.

There have been many stories about how some cities, especially smaller ones, gathered their revenue. At one time, most small towns and rural areas with a very small tax-base, paid their officers and other officials, from the fines collected on traffic violations and other offenses.

Most of these small towns had a justice of the peace who acted as judge and the police department was a town constable. Many of these JP's had no law degree, he was just some influential citizen. And the constable had no police training, and sometimes, not even a high-school education.

When a citation was issued and the person went before the JP, the fine was split between the JP, the Officer, or constable, and a small percentage to the town coffers. So one can imagine how many people were ever found *not guilty* in this scenario. I have heard of cases where these local law-enforcement characters would create situations to entrap motorists. The poor driver from out of town or out of state didn't have a chance. They would do things like allowing bushes and shrubs to grow up in front of stop signs so the driver couldn't see it until too late to stop. Or the one traffic light in town would have such a short amber phase he would not be able to stop before the light turned red. And it didn't matter to these people who you were. They just wanted your money.

One of my father's cousins was driving through a small community such as this in Mississippi in the fifties with his wife and kids in the car. He got just outside of town and heard gunshots. He looked in his mirror and saw an old, beat-up pickup truck with a small red light hanging from the rear view mirror. The driver, who turned out to be the town constable, was waving him over. He was driving his personal vehicle, with no siren and only the small red light. He accused this cousin of some minor infraction and when he didn't stop for the small red light, this keeper of public safety, started shooting. Knowing that cousin, I was surprised this poor excuse for a police officer didn't get a little training, or re-training, on the spot.

While working as a police officer, a friend of mine from a smaller city on the edge of the city where I worked, was on vacation with his wife driving through the state of New Mexico. He was stopped by a State Trooper for doing a few miles over the speed limit. We were quite accustomed to allowing a little tolerance in such cases in our departments, as long as the driver was not driving recklessly, so Frank thought other departments did the same.

In making conversation with this officer Frank asked him "are you state police or a highway patrolman?" The trooper slammed his citation book closed and said "you follow me back to town."

When they got back to the small town, they went before a justice of the peace. The trooper told his story of Franks violation and then said "and your honor, this man called me a highway patrolman."

The JP then pronounced sentence of a fifty dollar fine. Frank said "your honor, I'm also a police officer. Is there any way you could reduce the fine?" The JP then asked "are you on official business?" When Frank told him that he and his wife were on vacation he then said "in that case the fine is a hundred dollars."

This is how things were done, and can still be done, when no effort is made to select only the best and then train them constantly. This can be true in most any job. Not just law-enforcement. Especially positions of authority of any kind. I have had occasions to visit city offices for paperwork or permits or to renew auto tags and such where even the file clerk would look down her nose at you. Some can be very rude.

And now the socialists have convinced a lot of people that our police should be *de-funded*. This will only exacerbate the situation. With less funding, there will be less effort put into background checks, with less chance of finding qualified people. This will result in lower caliber police officers thus making the situation even worse. Of course this is just what the socialists want. They can heap on even more criticism and call for more de-funding. People need to wake up. Insist on better hiring practices along with more and better training. Continued training. Our police need our support. Not our criticism.

In most cases, when an individual is injured or killed, it's because he did something stupid. He resists the officer, attacks the officer (usually with a weapon) or runs. People need to learn that, if they are not guilty, the place to dispute the charge is in court, and most of them know this, so it seems pretty obvious they resist because they are guilty. With today's liberal judges they stand a better than average chance of being turned loose in court. But, if one takes the time to look into the background of this type of person, they will find a long criminal record. Why should he be considered a choir boy just because he caused the situation to turn deadly?

AMERICAN MANUFACTURING

America was built on the talents, ingenuity and hard work of the people. There was a time when the phrase "Made in USA" meant you had a quality product.

Unfortunately, that doesn't always hold true anymore. The "money hogs" don't care a hoot about quality, customer satisfaction, customer service or the customer's happiness. Their only concern is the bottom line, and this is understandable to an extent because they must answer to the stockholders.

So many products are now made with the cheapest materials, by the cheapest process possible. Many of their workers pick up on this attitude and perform shoddy work, with no concern for quality. Add to this, the "diversity hiring" rules with no concern for whether or not a person is qualified for the job or even wants to work if given the job.

This seems to be the norm for most products in today's world. Everything from automobiles to watch batteries, to insecticides.

I find batteries now have a very short life-span

compared to a few years ago. Cell phone batteries are exploding or causing fires. Our light bulbs would make Thomas Edison ashamed.

Most insecticides, claiming to be environmentally friendly, are so watered-down the only way they will actually kill a bug is to put enough on it to drown him. Or, worse yet, only kills the good insects. Resulting in destruction of the environment.

During WWII, our military personnel in the South Pacific regions were totally overwhelmed by flys and mosquitoes until a fantastic insecticide, called DDT, came along. It did a great job there and after the war it was made available here at home. All of our homes in the lowlands of West Tennessee were sprayed with it and we were not bothered with insects for months. I'm not sure if the service was provided by the county, the state or federal government but the people doing the work were driving military-surplus vehicles.

The DDT then became available to the public. It was very efficient and no doubt sales of other insecticide products became almost non-existent. Strangely enough someone decided DDT could cause cancer. Of all the hundreds of people whose homes were sprayed, I never heard of anyone having cancer or any adverse effects.

No doubt, all companies need to keep close tabs on their expenses and their bottom line but something so many of us find offensive is their outsourcing everything to other countries. They have their product made in places where the workmanship is questionable and sell it to us at huge profits. It's well known that the labor costs are much lower in third world nations. Twenty-five cents per hour is far more attractive than ten dollars per hour. And, even worse, in some cases it's child labor.

To make things even worse, they also outsource their customer service. When we encounter a problem and find it necessary to call for help, we call an 800 number that connects us with someone who can barely speak English. They can't understand the caller any better than we can understand them.

A few years back I found it necessary to call about a problem with my computer, a major brand. When I made contact with this so-called customer service rep, he could not speak so pretty good English and was also rude. He seemed to be not really interested in my problem and after several minutes of trying to make him understand me and trying to decipher what he was saying, I became frustrated, called him a cute name and hung up. He called me right back and said *"you called me an A**$@le"*. I said "yes, because you are an A**$@le" and hung up a second time. I swore never to use that brand of computer again.

Shoddy materials and workmanship seems to be the norm any more. When I retired from a company that is one of the biggest names in the manufacture of medical equipment and supplies, many of the items were being rejected at a rate of fifty percent or more, due to poor workmanship.

Quite a few years ago, I made the observation that the only thing in the workplace anymore, that has to be absolutely correct, is the paycheck.

Automobiles have become one of our most needed possessions, and the most expensive, other than our home. It's expensive because of several things.

First of all, auto workers are some of the highest paid workers in the U. S. counting hourly wages, and all sorts of fringe benefits not available to most other workers. Of course they have their unions to *extort* such goodies from the auto companies which the corporations pay to avoid being shut down by strikes.

Today's automobiles are loaded with every type of electronic device imaginable. Electronic ignition systems Electric windows and door locks, GPS systems, cameras to look in all directions, air bags and seat belt reminders. Under the hood is a multitude of gadgets and gizmos that I'm convinced, serve no real purpose but they are integrated into the system in such a way the vehicle will not run properly when they go bad. To me these are just extra parts sales. To make it worse the average Joe can no longer work on his own car because special equipment and tools are needed to do the most minor repair.

So many products are now manufactured overseas, including many medications, that we have to wonder if *anything* is made here. It's a blessing for those countries, I'm sure, but what about those Americans who want to work but are unemployed because their former employer downsized and sent their job to one of those countries with cheap labor? Or is it because too many American workers have developed the "don't care attitude"?

Let's put America to work first.

One of the greatest threats to the American people is the food supply. Most people today would have a very difficult time trying to grow a simple back-yard garden. Grocery stores have made it far too convenient for people to obtain food for the family. Mom can just stop off at her favorite supermarket and grab something quick and easy for dinner on the way home from work, or if time is really limited, she can swing by a fast-food location for burgers or a pizza. Cholesterol city.

But, the danger goes much deeper than what to grab in a hurry. Almost every type of fruit or vegetable has been hybridized by the giant seed companies. Their claim is they are making them grow faster and bigger and are able to feed more people. What they don't tell people is the fact that seeds cannot be saved from any of today's plants and planted next year.

If you wish to grow those nice tomatoes, beans, cucumbers or cantaloupes next year, you are *forced* to go back to the seed companies for more seed. Of course the seed prices keep going up. One of my brothers has a small farm and grows several types of vegetables. For quite a few years now he has grown a sweet corn and the cost has steadily increased. The cost is now something like twenty-five dollars per pound. The same is true for cantaloupe, or you can buy a pack of twenty seed for a mere nine dollars. The farmers pay hundreds of dollars a bushel for seed to grow soy beans or cotton and I am told the soy bean seed *can* be planted the next year but the seed companies managed to *buy* a law that makes it a criminal offense to do so.

In their efforts to make the plants grow more quickly and increase profits, they sacrifice flavor and also quality. There have been several reports on the loss of the actual food value and one report indicated that the nourishment value is something like sixty percent of what is was about fifty years ago.

It seems many of these hybridized plants don't have the ruggedness or adaptability to withstand adverse weather conditions like normal plants created by God and nature. Far too much of what the plants produce rots on the vine before picking time. Growing up on a farm was hard work but we almost never had to use insecticides or fertilizers and we grew some great crops.

The scary thing about this picture is the possibility of a year of widespread crop failures or the ever-possible loss of our power grids. Either one can, very quickly, bring about empty store shelves and a lot of hungry people. In such a scenario, no home will be safe.

No doubt these dangers don't worry the money-hogs at the seed companies. They will satisfy themselves by counting their millions. If a disaster does come about that causes a food shortage, the seed company big shots can demand *any* price for their seeds.

THE WORK FORCE VS WELFARE

"Democracy will cease to exist when you take away from those who are willing to work and give to those who would not".

Thomas Jefferson

Throughout most of our history, the American people have been industrious, hard working individuals. However, in 1935 Franklin Roosevelt started a program called *"The New Deal"* in which he incorporated a system of welfare. The nation was just coming out of the great depression and a lot of people were still out of work and this was supposed to *help* them get back on their feet. Instead, it helped a lot of them to get back on the couch.

Today, we have multitudes who go from cradle to grave without once holding down a full time job and they feel this is not only normal and okay but is owed to them. They don't realize it's part of the socialist plan.

The workforce; the people who go to work every day, to support their families and also those deadbeats who feed at the *public trough*. Unfortunately, that group known as the American worker is shrinking while the number living off the tax dollar is rapidly increasing. The last figure I heard was something like forty-six percent of the population is supporting the rest. That percentage is probably even less now. Why?

Consider this. The people who work must buy their own health insurance. If they have a family, they have to buy family insurance, home-owner's insurance, auto insurance, house payments and car payments. Many have piled up debts in the form of student-loans in order to educate themselves in hopes of finding a job that will allow him, or her, to afford all these obligations and still pay the taxes expected of them, so much of which goes to take care of the deadbeats. Too often their job doesn't pay enough to cover it all, they slide deeper into debt and end up having to take on a second job or try to get overtime. The extra work obligates them to pay even more taxes, It has been obvious to me for some time that our society encourages people to be bums. The more one tries to improve his lot, the more he is penalized. When one works the extra job(s) he pays more taxes. If he does improvements on his home, it's evaluated higher and requires more taxes. College tuition for his kids.

Most working people realize the hardships and expense of raising a family and usually have one or two children, sometimes three. Some choose to have none

The parasites have no such concerns, having one child after another. In fact, the more they have, the more government assistance is eagerly heaped upon them. The more kids they have, the more the rewards. Welfare, food stamps (EBT), aid-to-dependent-children (ADC) with payments actually beginning before the child is even born. Free pre-natal care, and free hospital-delivery. Then come all the free handouts of baby food, diapers and baby clothes.

And, as if this is not enough reward, these same people who go all year without working or paying any taxes, are encouraged to file a tax return as "head-of-household" for the "earned income credit" wherein they receive hundreds, even thousands in a tax refund on taxes they never paid. How can an individual who has no *earned income* receive an earned-income-credit? But, the poor working people, who have been paying taxes all year, and probably doing without a lot of things they need, usually end up paying even more taxes at tax time. Maybe *earned income credit* is another way of saying "buying the vote". Do you think?

Although these parasites receive food stamps and a welfare check every month, their kids are given free breakfast and free lunch at school (when they show up).

Most cities also have Food Banks to "feed the needy". When holidays roll around there is a tremendous push, food-drives if you will, to, you guessed it, "feed the needy". Hundreds, even thousands of food baskets are put together at Thanksgiving and Christmas, along with toy-drives. I noticed this past Christmas, there are groups begging for Christmas *gifts* for children around the world. This sounds very noble but many of those nations don't believe in Christmas, Santa Claus or God.

When school lets out for the summer there are many concerns about the kids going hungry without the free breakfasts and lunches at school. What have the parents done with the welfare and food stamps they've been getting each month? It's a known fact that some sell their food stamps for alcohol money or maybe even drugs. Made a *little* more difficult with EBT cards.

Does anyone ever ask the poor working sucker if his kids are hungry or if they have toys? Probably not. He's not likely to sell his vote.

"The folks who are getting free stuff, don't like the folks who are paying for the free stuff, because the folks who are paying for the free stuff can no longer afford to pay for the free stuff and their own stuff.

The folks who are paying for the free stuff want the free stuff to stop and the folks who are getting the free stuff want even more free stuff on top of the free stuff they are already getting.

Now...the people who are forcing the people to pay for the free stuff, have told the people who are receiving the free stuff, that the people who are paying for the free stuff, are being mean, prejudiced and racist.

So...the people who are getting the free stuff have been convinced they need to hate the people who are paying for the free stuff, by the people who are forcing some people to pay for the free stuff and giving them the free stuff in the first place.

The number of people getting the free stuff now outnumber the people paying for the free stuff".

Edward R. Murrow

Now and then we hear news-reports, from one public agency or other, saying that the latest study shows that a certain percentage of workers are not saving enough for their future. They don't have adequate savings or investments to cover emergencies or their retirement. Is there any wonder? Of course the parasites have no such worries. The government (politicians) will take care of them, their entire lives, for a few votes.

By not having a job to show up for and not having to worry about missing a paycheck (welfare), these bums have lots of time to take part in demonstrations, shut down streets and bridges, to complain and demand more freebies or more of anything they can think of.

Our Constitution, Amendment I, gives people the right to "peaceably" demonstrate but it does not say it's ok to disrupt business, interfere with public commerce or stop traffic, nor does it give people the right to destroy property. That's called "anarchy" and there are laws against such activity but officers are not allowed to arrest in so many instances.

Too often when people have a grievance and go out to express their right to demonstrate there are a lot radicals and hoodlums who join in and turn a peaceful demonstration into acts of violence or a riot, while making believe they are on the side of the ones who are there with a grievance.

Many of these trouble makers are there at the request and direction of left-wing liberals or other enemies of the country. They show tremendous anger and threats of further violence knowing so many of the government officials will grant their wishes to avoid violence…. or to avoid losing a vote.

CONUNDRUM
Something that is puzzling or confusing

Six conundrums of socialism in the United States of America

1. America is called Capitalist and greedy – yet half the population is subsidized.
2. Half the population is subsidized – yet they think they are victims.
3. They think they are victims – yet *their* representatives run the government.
4. Their representatives run the government – yet the poor keep getting poorer.
5. The poor keep getting poorer – yet they have things people in other countries only dream of.
6. The poor have things people in other countries only dream of - yet they want America to be more like those other countries.

Think about it! That pretty much sums it up in the USA in the 21st century. Makes you wonder who is doing the math.

Another one worth considering……

Seems we constantly hear about how Social Security is going to run out of money, but we never hear about Welfare or food stamps running out of money. ?? What's interesting is the first group "worked for their money" but the second group didn't (and won't). Think about that.

If you need a gun and don't have one…You'll probably never need one again.

Thanks to my old Army buddy Jack Percy.

THE RIGHT TO VOTE

"Use it or Lose it"

In many parts of the world, the citizens don't have the right, or privilege, of voting for their, so-called leaders. In some countries they *are* allowed to vote but only for one person…the dictator who, naturally, always wins.

It took a lot of effort, and hard work, to bring about voting rights for all American citizens but today all of us can vote who are of voting age. Unfortunately so many don't bother to do so. Like voicing their opinions in letters or phone calls to their elected officials or letters to their local paper, people say "I'm only one person. My one vote won't matter".

Someone made the well-known statement "People deserve the government they vote in". Perhaps we can add to that phrase "the government *allowed* to be voted in because we didn't vote". If the decent, hard-working people don't take responsibility and do our part, we can expect our country to be destroyed by radicals, and they are working very hard to do so, and constantly.

There are some people today who consider the vote so valuable they commit voter fraud. They find ways to vote in more than one precinct or even more than one state. It's unbelievable how many people are able to vote who have been deceased for years. Some localities never purge their voter roles.

Just as disturbing, if not more so, is the number of illegals who find a way to vote. No doubt that's why the liberals want open, uncontrolled borders. Statistics tend to show that aliens who get the opportunity to vote, do so mostly as democrats. The figures have been reported to be anywhere from eighty to ninety-five percent. I'm sure they have heard the liberals' promise of free everything. The land of milk and honey.

Knowing these facts, there are many cities, counties and states who declare themselves "sanctuaries" for illegals and also refuse to purge their voter roles. Some have more names on their voter roles than the number of residents in the county of voting age.

And yet, so many object to a requirement for any type of voter ID. They claim it puts a burden on the poor. That's bovine-feces. There is almost no one in today's world who doesn't have several forms of ID. But it's so much easier to commit voter fraud if one does not have to *prove* who they really are.

A February 2012 Pew Report found that 1.8 million deceased registrants were listed as "active voters" and that 2.75 million voters had registrations in more than one state. Obama's attorney general, Eric Holder told MSNBC that voter fraud *"simply does not exist to the extent that would warrant voter ID laws"*.

Now there is a tremendous push to make it legal to vote by mail. No doubt this will make it easier for deceased registrants to vote. Our nation is in serious trouble and, it seems very few people are paying attention. Our enemies are relentless.

EDUCATION SYSTEM

"If you can read this, thank a teacher"

Our education system has, perhaps, been among the best in the world, with the basics being provided without cost for the most part. Even though there is no real provision for it in the Constitution it was deemed to be a good idea. I am very happy this has been so, but now the socialists seem to be in control of the schools.

Today there are private schools and religious schools as well as the public schools. While attending school, in a small two-room public school, we started each day with the pledge of allegiance to the Flag. We would take turns reading a few verses from the Bible, perhaps sing a hymn or a patriotic song. Today this would probably bring law suits against the school system and, no doubt, the teacher would be fired.

I never heard of any student, or any parents, who considered this to be harmful. We also studied American History and geography. All this taught us love and respect for our country and our fellow man. It also taught us morals.

It would be interesting to see some statistics which compare the percent of students from those times who got into trouble to the numbers of today who end up in jail, get on drugs or in other trouble. I recall seeing a bumper sticker recently that says it all. *"They took prayer out of the schools and now the jails are full"*

No doubt the teachers of today hope to give every child a good education and I'm sure many teachers love their pupils almost as their own children but they are so restrained in what and how they can teach. It's my understanding that American History and geography are not considered so important anymore.

An atheist woman by the name of Madelyn Murray O'Hair (04-13-19 to 09-29-95) brought an end to prayer in school with a lawsuit against the school system in 1962. The case went all the way to the U. S. Supreme court which ruled in her favor. The Chief Justice of the supreme court in 1962 was Earl Warren. She was dubbed the most hated woman in America by Life Magazine.

O'Hair waged her war against Christianity in America for thirty years. In 1995 she, her son John Garth Murray and her granddaughter, Robin Murray O'Hair disappeared from San Antonio, Texas along with some $500,000 in gold coin. In January 2001 the FBI discovered the three burned, dismembered bodies on a remote S/W Texas ranch. A man by the name of David Roland Waters, her employee, was charged with the murders. I have often wondered to whom she prayed when she realized she was about to die.

It seems that the left wing Socialists are hell bent to do away with anything to do with Christianity or God in America. This nation was founded on Christianity, not religion. Almost all of our founding fathers were Christians and there is a lot of evidence to the fact. The Ten Commandments are built into and displayed on many public structures but the left-wing radicals hope to totally eradicate them. I don't believe it will happen.

Edmund Burke: Jan 12, 1729 – Jul 9, 1797, an Irish statesman, praised by both conservatives and liberals, was considered the *founder* of modern conservatism. He considered Christianity to be "a vehicle of social progress". He stated *"The only thing necessary for the triumph of evil is for good men to do nothing"*.

It is stated that the Democratic rule is *"the majority rules"*. According to statistics, something like eighty-six percent of the people believe in God. That means approximately fourteen percent don't believe in God. Of that fourteen percent, it's probably just a small percentage who actually complain and try to remove any semblance of Christianity. So that means, a really small percentage of the people are able to control the rest of us. That's NOT Democracy.

"Democracy is two wolves and a lamb voting on what to have for lunch…. Liberty is a well-armed lamb contesting the vote". *Benjamin Franklin*

Not only has Christianity been removed from our schools but another segment of the Communist manifesto has been fulfilled. The left wants to eradicate our borders and totally erase Christianity and the American way of life. The truly sad part is they have a lot of help from natural born citizens who have been brain washed.

For many years now, government has dictated the

school curriculum. The teachers must teach those subjects dictated and in the fashion prescribed. Too bad parents don't take a stand.

Our colleges are even worse, with so many left-wing professors it makes you wonder if they can do anything with their right hand. The very first radical known to man is known as Lucifer, aka Satan. Unfortunately, he has many disciples, his children, to carry on his work and many of them are now in our government where they can do the most harm.

"We have staked the whole future of America's civilization, upon the capacity of each and all of us to govern ourselves according to the Ten Commandments"
James Madison

School days should be, not only educational, but also one of the happiest parts of a child's life. I can say that mine were. It was such a joy to go to school that I can remember getting upset when the weather was too bad to walk the two miles or so to school. I loved just about all my teachers throughout my school days. Except a couple of college professors in the sixties. There was so much to learn and my teachers had the knowledge.

We were taught patriotism and allegiance to the Flag and the Constitution as well as appreciation for the freedoms and opportunities not found in other nations. We were not taught that we were owed anything from our government other than the freedom to choose.

I fear we have allowed the liberals to control our education systems far too long. Due to their slow, patient, determined way of brainwashing our young people they have converted many of our citizens into enemies of their own Nation. Much like the method of "boiling a frog". You don't toss him into hot water. He would jump out. "You put him into cold water and slowly increase the heat". The heat is now almost unbearable folks.

I believe defending our Constitution is more easily accomplished with our vote than in a shooting war. If we can get the votes counted properly, and **honestly**.

COMMON SENSE

"Not so common anymore"

Quite often we hear it said these days, "common sense is not so common anymore". Perhaps it's because our young people are spending far too much time with a computer, tablet or cell phone. Most any place you go you see even the smallest kids playing games on one device or another. Part of the cause could be that parents are too busy to do things with their children to help them learn how to find solutions to problems. Mental exercises. Any kind of family activity is better than too much time on a computer. Computer knowledge is quite important in today's high-tech world but there is no substitute for quality family time. Go fishing.

It seems that stupidity is running rampant in our society. It has been called a "psychopathic nation" and if one pays close attention to the daily news reports that would seem to be the case. The news media treat the acts of crime and stupidity quite casually, as normal, sane behavior. They are just poor, misunderstood youth.

Unfortunately, the affliction is not confined to the criminal world. People still smoke in bed, leave children or pets locked in hot cars, text while driving, etc. etc. Perhaps much of this has been brought on by excessive use of drugs and alcohol. Or, poor parental training.

Perhaps some of it is peer pressure to do wrong instead of doing what's right.

When growing up, people of my age had a lot of peer pressure; from extended family and friends but mostly from loving parents who would beat hell out of us if we did wrong. Stupidity was strongly criticized, not encouraged.

A recent news report points out the lack of common sense on the part of some young people today. On March 4, 2020, on Dunn Ave. in Memphis, Tn four individuals approached a home shortly after midnight. They were apparently oblivious to a neighbor's security camera across the street which recorded the entire episode.

The brilliant souls first threw a Molotov cocktail, a firebomb, against the house, which authorities believed was to draw the twelve occupants outside for act two.

They backed off a short distance and all four opened fire on the home with handguns, which, no doubt, were all registered and legal. Yeah, right.

Somehow, with twelve people inside, only one person was injured. A four-year-old child was struck in the leg. Police recovered approximately thirty shell-casings. But where the common sense really shines, one of these choir boys went home and called the police to report that one of his guns had been stolen.

The video footage from across the street showed him as one of the shooters and he was still wearing the same clothes. The video also showed his car, which a friend was driving, pull up to the curb to pick them up.

Sheer brilliance.

Reminds me of a call I was sent on when I was a police officer. An individual looking for some quick money decided to rob a bar and the few patrons inside. This was what was known as an "Okie Bar". Most of the patrons were from places like Texas, Arkansas and Oklahoma. These were people who were quite familiar with guns of all types.

Our hero in this case had only a cap gun, a toy, but obviously didn't think anyone would notice in the dim light. That was his second mistake. A few of the patrons took matters into their own hands and proceeded to give him a short course in bar-room etiquette. I have never seen a criminal so glad to see a police officer as this one was when I arrived.

I'm sure most any police officer in the country can relate numerous stories of this type of stupidity. There is more than enough to go around.

Another example of criminal brilliance, is how some will commit an armed robbery, or other crime, wearing bright green trousers and a yellow shirt, or such other bright colors. He can be seen six blocks away and you know he's your culprit. You gotta love 'em.

THE OBAMA YEARS

"Change you can believe in"

When I first heard the phrase, "*change you can believe in*", I thought, "If you come home and find your home burned to the ground, that's also change you can believe in".

The democrats could not bring themselves to ever be the least critical of Barak Hussein Obama. This was another individual, like Jimmy Carter, who was an unknown to most Americans, but with the help of the liberal, left-wing news media, he managed to acquire what is, arguably, the highest and most influential office on earth.

When first entering the political arena, in Illinois, the media immediately started showering him with accolades. He was charismatic, and charming; another John F. Kennedy, even. They started predicting he might become president. (Strange how that works).

Patriotic Americans started raising questions as to his origin of birth and his eligibility for that office. The democrats came to his rescue and started putting up smoke screens. He was everything they wanted. He was young, "charismatic", black and billed himself as a democrat.

He had made himself known to the liberal elites by being part of a neighborhood activist group, working with radicals in the streets. He was associated with Communist William Ayers, founder of "The Weather Underground", (and later made his way into our educational system). When people tried to investigate Obama's legitimacy to hold office as President of the United States, they ran into many roadblocks. It had been reported that he enrolled in college(s) as a foreign student, of Muslim religion and had received "foreign student aid" as such. When efforts were made to look into his college records, they found those *"sealed"*. Through a presidential decree no doubt.

A request was made for his birth record and it was not available or could not be found. After more than two years of questioning, a birth certificate was finally produced. This "certificate of birth" was examined by document experts who found several discrepancies and declared it a "forgery". But no one seemed to care. He was just what the socialists were looking for.

In one of his first speeches after taking office he stated "America is no longer a Christian nation. It is now a nation of Jewish, Muslim, Buddhist and Hindu and a nation of non-believers. His first year in office he did not *bother* to attend the National Prayer Breakfast, a tradition of presidents since 1953 when President Eisenhower attended, at the invitation of the Reverend Billy Graham.

Obama and the democrats claimed he was a Christian but after the pastor of the church he was attending, made national news demonizing and cursing America, he decided to change churches before it made him look bad to his supporters who had been fooled into voting for him.

He continued to try and pass as a Christian but made several blunders as time went by. In one speech or interview with a reference to religion, he made a slip and made reference to the "Holy Quran".

Even as far into his fake presidency as 2012, he was still showing his opposition to Christianity. The WWII Memorial Prayer Act, HR 2070, passed the House on 01-24-12. This was "To direct the secretary of the Interior to install, in the area of the WWII Memorial in the District of Columbia, a suitable plaque or inscription with the words that President Roosevelt had prayed with the nation on June 6, 1944. The morning of D-Day". Obama was opposed to it. Naturally.

The socialist democrats apparently felt that by having Obama in office they could have a field day. I'm sure they felt quite confident after having put him into office without having to prove his legitimacy or true legal status. The American people had taken the bait. The magic word "free" was put to work quite "freely".

A bill presented by Rep Rosa DeLauro (D-Ct) proposed free diapers for all the "needy", already being given a multitude of handouts. She suggested these could be dispensed through day-care centers.

Labor unions felt obliged to attack Boeing Aircraft and twenty-two "right-to-work" states, causing people to lose their jobs.

On March 23, 2010 Obama signed the fiasco called **"the affordable care act"** which meant it was affordable for those receiving welfare and food stamps as well as anything else they could finagle from a liberal government. Also for many illegal aliens.

For most working people the cost of insurance increased tremendously, and to make this bargain more painful, the act included a clause to penalize (fine) anyone who could not afford this bargain.

"Fathom the hypocrisy of a government that requires every citizen to prove they are insured...but not everyone must prove they are a citizen".

"Many of those who refuse, or are unable, to prove they are citizens will receive free insurance paid for by those who are forced to buy insurance because they are citizens".
Ben Stein

No doubt people frequently use words that are most familiar to them to express their views. In the Obama health care bill, page 107, appeared the word "Dhimmitude". If you google the word you will find that it is a Muslim word which exempts Muslims and certain "low-income" people from the requirement to buy this "affordable" insurance. No wonder it's called affordable.

When he was having trouble getting the debt ceiling raised in 2011, in order to deliver more freebies no doubt, he threatened to shut down several government programs. These were; Social Security payments, military retirements, social security disability and retirement checks for federal employees.

The payout programs he did NOT threaten; any payments to illegal aliens, welfare and food stamps, foreign aid and frivolous benefits like internet for violent offenders in prison. He did not threaten to remove any of the many federal employees he had hired or appointed nor to cut back on any freebies for his base voters.

From 2009 through 2010, under Obama, the ATF executed what was known as *Operation Fast and Furious* which allowed more than two-thousand firearms to "walk" across the U. S. border to Mexico, into the hands of the drug cartels. At least one of those guns was later used to kill a U.S. border patrol officer and, no telling how many other victims.

When the matter was investigated Obama and his attorney general, Eric Holder, denied any knowledge of the matter and Eric Holder lied to Congress about it. It's strange but no one was impeached, demoted or fired.

Obama was not only helped to worm his way into the White House, but surrounded himself with these left-wing conspirators, Nancy Pelosi being one of the worst.

Just over three-quarters of a century ago, Washington, DC was a fairly small, sleepy town. Now the DC area is among the wealthiest metropolitan areas in America. Six of the wealthiest ten counties in America surround Washington, DC.

The standard salary for members of Congress is a measly $174,000 per year. Their retirement can be up to eighty percent of that, depending on how long they can keep fooling their constituents. To top it off, they receive over ten-thousand dollars more of our tax dollars to *help* pay for their health insurance. And yet, they hope to do away with Social Security that the working people have been paying for all their working lives.

This comes to over two-hundred thousand per year for the average Congressman, for an exhaustive 124 days per year. And poor Nancy Pislosi, as speaker of the House, draws a mere $223,500. per year. With salaries like these, and they accomplish almost nothing, unless you count an attempted impeachment of a duly elected President. No wonder there's not enough revenue.

They draw exorbitant wages while the poor sucker paying their salary, does well to put food on his family's table. It's no wonder they try to hold on to their jobs as long as possible. Perhaps we need to insist on term limits. Better yet, these should be *voluntary* positions.

Members of Congress, when our nation was first founded, were mostly volunteers because the Country meant something to them. After Washington became president, they were paid. From 1789 to 1815 members of Congress were paid six dollars per day *while in session.* From 1818 to 1855 they were paid eight dollars per day.

It shows that when people are put into a position where they can vote on their salary, their fringe benefits and their retirement, there is almost no limit to what they will extort, embezzle or steal. No wonder it's called the Swamp. Many voters blindly and obediently vote for *"the party"* without looking into what the person stands for. That's like voting for that person because of the color of his hair or the shoes he wears. People need to realize; the Democratic party of today is not the Democratic party of our grandfathers'. The socialists have been working their way into more and more powerful positions and brainwashing our young people, in order to get control for decades now. They very patiently and quietly take their time in accomplishing their goals. The indoctrination of our school children being, perhaps, their greatest weapon.

One has to wonder, which of these fools thinks he or she will be the "comrade leader" if successful? Can you picture Hitlery Clinton or Nancy Pelosi as head of the American Communist Party? It's frightening.

Sadly, it's a possibility, because so many young people have already been brainwashed into believing that everything about America is wrong and has been so throughout our history. A Harris Poll found that almost fifty percent of voters under age forty, say they would rather live under socialism than capitalism (freebies). Needless to say, this all comes from the socialists within our educational system. They have produced generations of Americans who know almost nothing about their country, except that they hate it.

"The trouble with our liberal friends is not that they are ignorant; it's just that they know so much that isn't so".
Ronald Reagan

It's no wonder we can now be called a psychopath nation. The young people are being taught to rebel. They are encouraged to create social unrest. So much of it really took off in the sixties, during what was called "the hippie era". That's when the communist doctrines really started to come to the forefront. *"Get control of the schools. Get the young people interested in alcohol, sex and drugs".* The philosophy became "if it feels good, do it". They had no shame, just belligerence. They had no pride, just selfish ego. Their socialist educators felt confident enough to bring their teachings out into the open. As though it was normal.

Many of the left wing hippie type have made their way into our political system, eg; Bill and Hilary as well as many others. Obama's CIA director, John Brennan actually voted for a communist party candidate for president, Gus Hall of Minnesota, in 1976. And Obama puts him in as head of the CIA. Gus Hall was a four-time candidate under the "Communist Party USA (CPUSA) ticket. From the way things are looking at the moment, he would have a very good chance of winning if he ran today. And the young people don't realize they are being used to accomplish the goals of our enemies. Unfortunately, many parents are as brainwashed as the Kids. "Freedom's last generation"??? Maybe.

Both Obama and Hilary read, studied and used Saul Olinsky's book "Rules for Radicals" which he dedicated to Satan. Obama used the book for many of his governing strategies, and actually helped fund the Olinsky Academy. He also taught workshops there on the Olinsky methods. Is there any wonder why our nation is falling apart? I strongly fear that, if we end up with just one more, mostly democratic administration, it will be the end of the America we know and, many of us, dearly love. We must find and elect more people who care about this great nation and are not pushing the socialist agenda. The Communist Manifesto.

PRESIDENT DONALD JOHN TRUMP

"Make America Great Again"

For the first time in many years, perhaps other than Ronald Reagan, we have a president who is not a career politician. Someone with the business expertise to make the tough decisions on our economy as well as foreign trade agreements. Unlike so many of his predecessors, he obviously loves America and the American people. And for the first time since Ronald Reagan, I feel that we have a president that I can refer to as "My President".

His winning the election came as a great surprise for the liberals who were convinced that Sweet Hilary, their queen, had it sewed up. There was much weeping and wailing. Within twenty minutes after he was sworn in, the Washington Post headline (banner) read "THE CAMPAIGN TO IMPEACH TRUMP HAS BEGUN". The day after his inauguration, the left-wingers started talking impeachment. His only crime; beating Hilary.

His many successes in the first two-and-a-half years have caused panic among the liberals because he has gone against everything they dream of. They have criticized and objected to or lied about everything he has done.

Before leaving office Obama used every means at his disposal to discredit or block Trump's every effort. He had his National Security Agency doing wiretapping, eavesdropping on personal phones of anyone they could reach, the IRS was running amuck, disallowing any type of conservative organization tax-exempt status. Sadly, Obama has been out of office for more than three years now and he's still putting in his two-cents worth.

Obama's left wing Attorney General said, as a slam against President Trump, "when I hear these things about let's make America great again; I think to myself. Exactly when did you think America was great"? New York governor, Andrew Cuomo commented "We're not going to make America great again. It was never that great". They should try living in Cuba or Venezuela.

It's unbelievable that people born in this great land can spout such garbage. People who have had more privileges than most of us and acquired so much wealth and power, and yet, seem to have so much hatred for the country of their birth. Perhaps they think they acquired all of this through their own magical, God-like powers. I think they should be candidates for one-way tickets to Russia, Iran or Venezuela. I am more than happy to contribute to the cost of their tickets.

Not long after President Trump was inaugurated, one of the loyal followers of the democratic socialists, attacked a group of Republican Congressmen who were playing baseball in DC. Luckily there were some police Officers on the scene and the individual was brought down. He was identified as James Thomas Hodgkinson, a sixty-six year old man from Belleville, Il. No doubt a college student of the sixties or seventies. Congressman Steve Scalise, R-La, was critically injured.

The attacker's weapon of choice was a *gun*? But, how can that be? Democrats hate guns and want them all confiscated. Or perhaps the desire is to confiscate guns only from law-abiding citizens.

I believe that most people, especially those of a conservative nature, are Christian, law-abiding people who don't hold with violence. However, this does not seem to apply to the violent, radical followers of the socialist hopefuls.

There have been numerous reports where these bullies have attacked Trump supporters just for wearing the red MAGA cap or anything indicating their support. In 2017 a fifty-year-old man and a fifteen year old boy were attacked and beaten by left-wing hoodlums in Berkley, Ca for wearing red caps. Another fool was arrested for ramming his van into a voter-registration tent.

A retired NYC police officer was attacked in Nashville, Tn where he was celebrating his fiftieth birthday wearing a *red cap* with the words "Make 50 Great Again". The attacker in this case was not only a fool but, obviously couldn't read.

These reports have shown up in newscasts from many parts of the country. It appears that wearing anything appearing to celebrate President Trump really makes the radicals see red. I wonder when they will get their brown shirts?

No doubt this is to be expected when the leaders

of these well indoctrinated, brainwashed people are all constantly adding fuel to the fire with their words and actions. People don't realize, they're being used.

With their phony impeachment attempt as well as the constant criticism of everything the President does or says. They have caused a division of the American people not seen since the Civil War and yet they accuse the President of being divisive.

It's amazing how so many liberal politicians feel free to lie about, falsely accuse or even threaten people they oppose. Like the phony impeachment attempt against a duly elected president and the threat made by Senate Minority Leader, Chuck Schumer, D-NY, against Supreme Court Justices Neil Gorsuch and Brett Kavanaugh. His loving comment was *"I want to tell you Gorsuch; I want to tell you Kavanaugh: You have released the whirlwind, and you will pay the price. You won't know what hit you if you go forward with these awful decisions".* (March 5, 2020).

It's no wonder there are so many mental-midgets out there committing acts of violence and anarchy when their illustrious idols are constantly encouraging them to do so with their own acts of rebellion. It's my understanding that the people elected to high office are also required to take an oath of allegiance to America, the Constitution and the government that they are supposed to be part of. Not to overthrow it to form the type of government they think is best. Whether it be a socialist republic or Muslim state. To me such actions should be considered treason. Just that simple.

Many people were hoping Hilary Rodham Clinton would be elected president in 2016 but, fortunately, enough people saw her for what she is. Perhaps many remembered her failure to take the required action to save the lives of the Americans in Benghazi, Libya, but, instead ordered two branches of the military to *"stand down"* when they were about to go in and rescue our people. No doubt that was an indication of just what kind of president she would be.

Thank God enough people made the right decision in 2016 and we can only hope and pray that enough will be willing to brave the storms of Covid-19 and all the social disorder going on in 2020.

The liberals have opposed and criticized every effort President Trump has made to combat the Corona virus. First they tried to claim he didn't act soon enough, and when it was proven that he started taking action immediately, they tried to say it was too little too late or it was the wrong thing to do. Even when he made himself a guinea pig and took the Hydroxychloroquine vaccine, they criticized that. If he used a magic wand and made it all disappear tomorrow, it would be the wrong color wand or some other dumb complaint.

President Trump is not a career politician and owes no favors. He has the intestinal fortitude to do what needs to be done and doesn't care if it does ruffle their feathers. I shudder to think what condition our nation would be in right now, with all that's going on, if any one of his predecessors was in office. He does what needs to be done without regard for politics. He could have accomplished more if he had some help.

The President in our past history, who most closely faced similar problems and similar foes, was Andrew

Jackson, "Old Hickory". He found DC full of corruption and also had many detractors or enemies. He, too had a strong love for the nation and it's people, believed strongly in the Union but with less government interference in the lives of the citizens. He felt the primary duty of federal power, once invoked, was to protect the many from the few. *Amen.*

Jackson had several occasions in which he found it necessary to fire and replace some officials. Some saw such actions as the ruin of the country. Jackson saw it as the nation's salvation.

Jackson was president from 1829 to 1837 and we only had twenty-four states at the time he took office. He fought the British in the war of 1812 as a Major General, which is when he was given the nickname of "Old Hickory". He was ready to face down any enemy and was ready to defend his friends from any bad guys. He was wounded in a frontier-style gunfight and then tried to physically assault his would-be assassin. He thought of himself as a father figure and the people as his family. *See the book "AMERICAN LION" by Jon Meacham.

The liberals and the left-wing media have a total, even vulgar, hatred for President Trump. Never in my eighty-five years on earth have I seen such complete disrespect for the nations President. Of course the people have been brain-washed into disrespecting him, his office and the nation itself. That's because there is criticism of everything he does and says. When people hear a lie often enough and long enough, it becomes the truth, no matter how false.

When President Trump had our military take out Iran's monster general, Quassem Soleimani, instead of any positive reporting of the action, the left-wing news media were mostly critical, as we might expect.

MSNBC referred to it as "Trump's Benghazi" but they had no criticism of Hilary Clinton when her debacle there cost the lives all Americans in the embassy. The Washington Post called Soleimani Iran's "most revered" The New York Times tweeted a video of Soleimani reciting poetry and compared him to Martin Luther King.

NBC correspondent, Richard Engel, stated "The U.S. officially classified Soleimani as a terrorist, but Iran considered him a national hero". *We should care?* To shower more praise upon this demon Engel described him as "smart, charismatic, ruthless, strategic and bold. His power made Iranians proud". He received similar accolades from CNN, CBS and others. Sounds like most U.S. news agencies were also proud of him.

Time Magazine went so far as to say "parents should tell their children he was "a top military leader in Iran, a country in the Middle East"

Hollywood stars apologized to Iran and filmmaker Michael Moore actually wrote a letter of apology to the supreme leader of Iran. He should be charged with a crime.

Former NFL activist, Colin Kaepernick called the elimination of one of America's worst enemies "racist". He said " there is nothing new about American terrorist attacks against black and brown people for the expansion of American imperialism". Sounds like a comment straight out of the Kremlin. Can one believe such garbage? Why does he not move to Iran? Perhaps because they won't pay him millions of American dollars to play ball. And these people are what our children and young people have to look up to as role models? As heroes? I know the socialists are wetting their pants with joy.

President Trump has suggested suspending the payroll tax until the economy improves, in order to increase the pay of American workers. But, Nancy Pelosi wants to provide a trillion dollars to the cities and states where poor management has put them into near bankruptcy…. and, on top of that, she wants to *"provide a guaranteed income for all"*, while Bernie Sanders wants *Medicare for all*. How many votes will that buy?

Would this guaranteed income replace welfare or be in addition to it? The bigger question is, where will all this money come from? Will this come from the 70% tax rate they hope to impose on the working people by way of the *"Green New Deal"*? The "Green New Deal" will ban most air travel, and ban air conditioning in our homes. Would that include *their* homes?

In his book "The Big Lie", Dinesh D'Souza states that" in both ideology and tactics, the American left is rooted in fascism and Nazism, and its thuggery, censorship and intimidation tactics are part of a deliberate effort to subvert the democratic process just as Hitler and Mussolini did".

A list of short-term demands, in the Communist Manifesto; "a progressive income tax, abolishing inheritance and private property, free education, (for the brainwashing of our young, no doubt), nationalization of any means of transport (airlines, trucking industry, trains and busses), also communications, and centralization of credit by way of a national bank.

We already have one bill, passed in 1997, called the "Crime and Terrorist Bill" which allows the Feds to confiscate money and property of people deemed to be *Rebels* or who are trying to emigrate to another country. The good old IRS can confiscate our property without due process. All they have to do is show, or think, we owe taxes. They can write their own rules (legislate) and then take action (enforcement) and decide the guilt of the accused and levy a penalty (judicial). No wonder Obama was able to use them against his opponents.

President Trump has mentioned that abolishing the IRS might be a good idea. Of course the high-paid, left-wing royalty totally disagree, but then, they disagree with anything he says or does. They would love to convince people that he was the cause of the Corona virus. If we were hit with another ice-age, I'm sure he would be blamed for that as well.

From day one of President Trumps term in office, the left-wingers kept looking for any excuse to try and remove him. They were constantly cussing and discussing ways to impeach him. They made numerous accusations which were proven to be false. When one attempt would fail, they would look for another. For three years, or more, they continued to beat the drums until, finally, they received their ultimate wish. A letter from "an anonymous whistle blower" or so they say, and they began to cheer and attacked with the ferocity of a pack of hungry dogs.

For weeks they totally forgot, or ignored, all duties of the House of Representatives and tried, desperately, to build some kind of case around the phantom's letter. They refused to name the Whistler or to allow President Trump's team to call witnesses or put on any kind of defense. We can but wonder if the "whistle blower" was in their own midst or if the letter might have been fabricated by a team from their illustrious group. Surely not. After all, these are duly elected, honest, professional democrats. Yeah. Right.

The sixth Amendment of the Constitution states "the accused shall enjoy the right to a speedy and public trial by an impartial jury". Which was a joke in this case. The same amendment goes on to say "to be confronted with witnesses against him; to have compulsory process for obtaining witnesses in his favor, and to have assistance of council for his defense".

This "impartial Jury" allowed none of these rights or privileges, rushed through the proceedings "in order to be finished by Christmas" (2019). And then the illustrious, impartial House Speaker, Nancy Pelosi sits on the articles of impeachment for thirty-three days before passing them on to the Senate for trial. The entire process could not have been more partisan, one-sided and corrupt.

When this circus, or vaudeville show, reached the Senate floor, the House democrats insisted the Senate do the job they had failed to accomplish. When the Senate refused, the democrats said *they* were being partisan and "immoral". A group of people who fight for open borders, asylum for illegals. plus free benefits of every kind, and abortions-on-demand calling the senators *Immoral*. WOW!

When President Trump took the podium for his 2020 "State-of-the Union" address, on February 4th, it became immediately obvious how much hatred the House democrats felt for him. Most of the audience stood and applauded but the disappointed accusers showed no such respect, remaining seated with their venom showing in their scowling faces.

During the hour-and-a-half address the audience gave him a standing ovation numerous times but the sour grapes remained seated, scowling and shaking their heads negatively.

At the end of the President's address, as an example of her professionalism and respect for the office of president, the "impartial" House speaker, Nancy Pelosi, very casually and slowly and deliberately, ripped up her copy of the President's speech. A couple of pages at a time to drive home her disdain for him. I'm not sure if she was sober enough to really know what she was doing.

"Remember, democracy never lasts long. It soon wastes, exhausts and murders itself. There never was a democracy yet that did not commit suicide".

John Adams

Another deadly assault on our Constitution made during the false Obama era, was the disaster made in collusion with our enemies in the United Nations, known as the "Small Arms Treaty".

This is another liberal scheme to bring about, not just "gun control", but *international* gun control and gun registration. This would actually give foreign leaders a say in how our Constitution is interpreted and would require a "National Control List" (Article V of the treaty)….a record-keeping system to track end-users of small arms for a minimum of ten years. Needless to say, ten years of gun registration will lead to "gun confiscation". This would give foreign leaders control of who can and cannot own a gun.

This so-called "treaty" is stuck in the Senate but President Trump has asked that it be returned so he can dispose of it. However, not enough senators believe strongly enough in the Constitution to return it to the White House. I'm sure many of them are sitting on their laurels, just waiting to see how the 2020 election goes. If they can keep it alive until they get enough of their own breed in the Senate, the treaty will be signed.

We don't need any more influence from other nations. People who hate us and have every intention of destroying everything we stand for.

The people trying so hard to take away our guns are the same people wanting less military funding. They want the nation to have no defense of any kind; and now they are trying to de-fund and disarm our police officers. No doubt their next effort will be to disarm our military.

It seems that some people who voted for President Trump are now believing much of the left-wing propaganda. They are "not sure" if he's the right one for the job. Or they don't like his "public face".

Is he a bit crude? Perhaps. Is he outspoken? Yes. Is he sometimes a little vulgar? Yes. Is he what America needs? **Hell yes!** He is the first president in many years who is not a wimp or a left-wing radical. He has the courage (guts) to do what needs to be done for the nation. The socialists have criticized his foreign relations and trade-agreements along with everything else he has done or attempted to do. He realizes you can't bargain with a rattle snake. I'm sure the radicals would rather he deliver another plane load of cash to our enemies, as Obama did to Iran.

When I hear people talk about the President being crude or outspoken, I ask them "if your home is on fire and you only have dirty water to extinguish the fire, do you wait for someone to bring clean water?"

The fools who are trying so hard to destroy your liberties and mine don't have enough common sense to realize they are giving away their own. If the world's socialist are able to totally destroy our way of life and our government, they will have their own leaders ready to take over. The imbeciles who are working so hard to bring us down will, no doubt, be the first to be eliminated. All the freebies will be replaced with chains.

"They promise them freedom, but they themselves are slaves of corruption; for whatever overcomes a man, to that he is enslaved" 2 Peter 2:19 RSV

SOCIALISM IN AMERICA

If one takes a close look at American History, it becomes pretty obvious there has been a form of socialism creeping into our system of government for a long time. The communist manifesto was published, or made known to the public, around the 1840's. Some politicians found many of the ideas quite attractive and started trying to apply them.

These Bums have instituted changes quite slowly. A new tax here, a new law there, while telling us "this is for the benefit of the people". One of the more recent examples is the seat belt law. They claim it's to save lives, and it can, but I don't think forced compliance is allowed by the Constitution. It's for revenue.

When first put into law there was no penalty and officers were not allowed to stop a driver to see if he was wearing his seat belt. He could only issue a warning citation for it if you were stopped for some other infraction. And then they instituted a small fine, and then the fine was increased. Next came the push to have officers stop people if they *believed* they were not using the seat belt. Much like the method of boiling the frog.

Vladimir Lenin (1870 – 1924) was the founder of the Russian Bolsheviks and leader of the Russian Revolution. He was the first head of the U.S.S.R.

Around 1899 he put together and circulated a list of things they, the Communist, could do to destroy the United States of America.

This list of instructions included things like *"destroy the churches (Christianity), dilute the laws, get the young people interested in alcohol, sex and drugs, infiltrate the government"*, as well as other ideas. These things all fit in very nicely with the Communist Manifesto, which includes a lot of free stuff to make people dependent on government, and control of our schools in order to brainwash the young people.

There were also instructions from various other people.

"The first battlefield is to rewrite history...take away the heritage of people and they are easily persuaded." *Karl Marx*

Could that be called "Canceling America"?

****

"To destroy people you must first sever their roots." Aleksandr Solzhenitzyn

"The most effective way to destroy people is to deny and obliterate their own understanding of their history."

George Orwell

Can anyone deny that this has been happening for many years now? And our schools have been the primary tool to accomplish their goals. They have rewritten history and taught our young people to hate their own country. We have allowed it to happen.

Perhaps one of the biggest accomplishments of the socialists was brought about by Franklin D. Roosevelt. Whether he did it wittingly or unwittingly may be hard to say. Maybe a little of both.?? Either way, I'm sure the socialist, the world over, applauded.

The Nation was in the throes of the great depression of the late twenties and early thirties and I'm sure he felt that something had to be done. However, so many of the programs he instituted should have been given a lot more thought. He took us off the "gold standard" which created problems for our economy due to inflation. The welfare programs, meant to help people get back on their feet, should have been *temporary*. Some of the allotted funds should have been used for vocational training to help people find jobs. Instead, a lot of people made it their life-long avocation.

Please refer back to the quote *"Democracy will cease" by Thomas Jefferson* on page 55.

America has always been a nation of aliens. The nineteenth century brought a huge influx of Italians, Irish and German immigrants as well as many other nationalities. For the most part, these people came to America, as our founding fathers did, to find a better life.

They assimilated themselves into American culture, learned the language and tried very hard to become true Americans. They did not come here with the thought of destroying our country or changing it to the kind of country from which they had fled.

Today we have even more people trying to immigrate to our great country. Many of them are trying very hard to find a better life, just as immigrants of the nineteenth century did. But, far too many are "invaders"; enemies of America, here to destroy our way of life.

It's obvious to anyone who pays attention that so many of these invaders come here with great patience and perseverance, to infiltrate our society with their offspring and work their way into our government. (One of the doctrines of the communist manifesto is to infiltrate our government.

A perfect example of this tactic is the number of admitted socialist in the democrat party. Such characters as Alexandria Occasio Cortez and her Squad, Preet Bharara and one of the most dangerous, Kamala Harris. Like so many they are first or second generation off-spring who were born in America thus giving them citizenship status. Unfortunately, being born in America doesn't always make one an American.

Along with these, we have nut cases like Bernie Sanders, Elizabeth Warren, Susan Rice, Nancy Pelosi, Chuck Schumer and many others not yet so well-known but born in America and just as dangerous.

The first group, no doubt, have been taught by their parents, all the socialist ideals of their homeland. With this training being reinforced by the many socialists who have infiltrated our educational system for generations.

The second group are people who should know better. People who have obtained fame and fortune at the expense of the Nation and the people. But then, they have been brainwashed by the same educational system.

It's amazing how people, whether new to this nation or descendants of early Americans, can get elected into our political system, swear an oath of allegiance to America and to the Constitution, and immediately start trying to destroy both. Why is this allowed? Why are they not charged with lying under oath, dereliction of duty or worse?

They should be immediately removed from office, jailed or deported to one of the socialist countries they seem to love. I wonder what their punishment would be if they tried such subversive acts in any one of those countries that they seem to admire?

Obiden keeps using phrases like "the American way" or "working for the American people". He says "President Trump is a liar and un-American." These phrases actually sound more like he is describing himself. Hearing him trying to use patriotic words and phrases makes me want to regurgitate. From him they sound just plain phony. They *are* phony.

In my humble opinion, teaching or promoting socialism in America, especially in our schools, should be a crime of sedition, espionage and treason. This great Nation was built on Christian principles. The socialist hope to eradicate any signs of Christianity and all remnants of American History.

The American form of government has been observed, acclaimed, even envied, and commented on by people of other nations almost from the beginning.
Quite an interesting quotation comes from a French

diplomat, politician and historian. His name was Alexis de Tocqueville (1805 – 1859). Full name, Alexis Charles Henri Cle'rel, Conte de Tocqueville. He is well known for his four-volume analysis of the social and political system of the United States. It was titled "Democracy in America" written in the years between 1835 and 1840.

He stated *"The American Republic will endure until the day Congress discovers that it can bribe the public with the public's money."*

"We can state with conviction, therefore, that a man's support for absolute government, is in direct proportion to the contempt he feels for his country."

Thanks to The Heritage Foundation.

He also said *"Liberty cannot be established without morality, nor morality without faith."*

Strange how our founding fathers, and so many others, knew human nature and the nature of Satan's children well enough to predict the outcome over a hundred years ago.

The Congressional Record of 1963 shows the list of *communist goals.* At least half, or more, of these goals are being practiced or supported in America today. Socialist are being elected into our government at all levels, including the legislative branch and the judiciary.

They are working full time to destroy our democracy and the American way of life. For many years the socialist movement has been a silent revolution but, as they have gained ground, they have become more open and more vocal, as well as more violent. This has been made quite evident by the actions of groups like ANTIFA and Black Lives Matter (BLM) with their violence in major cities across America.

While working diligently to destroy democracy they have constantly screamed that President Trump and the Republican Party are destroying Democracy. Everything President Trump does for the American people, Biden says *"That's not the American way."* No doubt he means "that's not the way the socialist in America want it done."

Of all the world's religions, most leave the final choice or decision to the individual. Only two groups seem to insist on total domination, although there is the question whether these two groups are "religious", "political" or "just plain "dictatorial" in nature. The two groups of which I speak, are the socialist and the Muslims. To me, both are based on fanaticism rather than religion.

Many people think of socialism as *"political"* but their goal is nothing short of world domination and control, and they will use any means available to accomplish the task. Including politics and even subversion and violence.

The world seems to have more than its' share of people whose sole objective is to destroy anything decent and Christian. It's strange that people, who seem to be reasonably intelligent, can't see the long-term goals of the socialist and communist. Not to mention the Muslims who feel compelled to kill those of us who don't accept their creed or philosophies. Our enemies have now convinced many people that Israel is our enemy. Perhaps that is one reason our Nation is experiencing so many problems today. *(Gen. 12.3)*

POST ELECTION

Another day which will live in Infamy

The election of 2020 has been, no doubt, the most unlawful and tumultuous in U. S. history. With mail-in votes, ballot harvesting and hiding or outright destruction of votes.

To make it worse, the computer software program operating the voting machines, reportedly owned by the husband of House Speaker Nancy Pelosi, suddenly suffered a *glitch* during the wee hours of morning and *transferred* thousands of Republican votes to the democrat scoreboard. No doubt some colleges will want that software program to operate their football scoreboards.

Strangely enough, although not surprising, most, if not all, of these *glitches* occurred in cities and states with democrat governors and mayors. These are the same states and cities where the poll workers and vote counters were democrats; where republican observers were not allowed close enough to see anything and the pole officials claimed "everything was done honestly and fairly." Yeah, RIGHT!

One of my brothers was told by a friend that when he

cast his vote, one of these illustrious poll-watchers was looking over his shoulder (voter-watcher?) and she saw he had voted for President Trump. She said to him in a very rude tone, **"What did you vote for him for?"** She should have been removed from that job.

There is no way these demons will ever convince me that there are enough "Americans" who want socialism. I think we know what's in the hearts of most "true Americans". Sure, you have a certain number who are dyed-in-the-wool democrats (my daddy was a democrat, my granddaddy was a democrat) type who will blindly vote for a brick if it's on the ballot as a democrat. Plus you have a few who have been "brain-washed" and some hear only the magic word "FREE".

Then you add in the experts at voter fraud with mail-in, unsolicited votes and ballot-harvesting, along with machines operated by the socialist computer program that was used to steal the government from the people of Venezuela.

The so-called votes were then counted by people who are part of the Obiden team. When demands were made for recounts, who did the recounts? Yep. The same ones who cheated in the first place. No wonder they don't want examination of the voting machines. Of course the left-wing news media says "it's all fair and square." And they expect us to believe it.

For many years we have seen them lie to our young people, or anyone else who will listen and believe their tripe. Now we have seen them steal an election through bribery, promises of free stuff, rigging voting machines, adding votes to their side and destroying votes of the opposition.

Naturally they deny any wrongdoing but, then, our prisons are filled with people who denied committing their crimes, even when caught on surveillance cameras or seen by eyewitnesses.

The socialist have stolen Venezuela, confiscated all guns and, by all indications, have enslaved the people.

If you google the Venezuelan dollar, it shows 100 Cien Bolivares (above) is now worth zero in American dollars.

It seems they are about to do the same routine in the United States.

I have heard people say, both before and since the election, "God is still in control", or "God will provide." I have no doubt that is true but I don't believe that God's Grace is like a welfare program, that we can sit on the couch, watch TV and wait for it to arrive in the mail.

He gave us a brain and two hands. He gave us two eyes to see what's going on around us, two ears to hear the propaganda and a mouth to speak out. We were given the brain to sort out the good from the bad and to decide what action we need to take. We are now in quite desperate need of action. Another election is coming....unless the socialist are able to eradicate that also. **GO VOTE!**

We must all learn to do our own thinking, do our own research. We must learn to recognize falsehoods and, most of all, learn to recognize the disciples of Satan who walk among us spreading their fertilizer and making impossible promises.

It appears the socialist have taken full control of our government and almost none of our elected "leaders" raised a hand or raised a voice in opposition. To make it worse, our military leaders seem to be accepting the "coup d' tat".

This is the scenario that has troubled me since Obama was allowed to take the White House without any proof of qualification. I wondered just what our military leaders and high-ranking law enforcement would do. It now appears they are willing to allow total destruction of our Constitution and our Nation. They are not abiding by their oath to uphold and protect the Constitution. To "Protect and Serve".

This was, without the slightest doubt, the most corrupt, illegal and frightening election in our history. In the states and large cities controlled by democrats, the liberal media started predicting, almost immediately, with only a small percentage of the votes counted, that the democrats were winners. Maybe they knew what was planned at the polls.

When the illustrious vote-counters decided to shut down for the night, President Trump was ahead by several thousand votes. But, strangely enough, when they continued the next morning, the vote-fairy had made a gift of several thousand votes during the night which put Obiden waaayy ahead. Are we really supposed to believe that?

Next came the infamous "glitch" in the software-story. That's how they tried to explain it but somehow Obiden (Obiden as in Obama) remained in the lead. These vote counters/falsifiers would only allow observers in after a court order and not for several hours even then. The observers who were allowed in were not permitted close enough to know if they were counting votes or letters from home.

Today's democrats should be ashamed to use or claim the word democrat or anything pertaining to "Democracy". Of course you can't expect any shame from people who have no shame and no conscience. To them democracy is being allowed to do any crooked thing they wish to with no objection from the wronged.

An even greater insult, not only to President Trump, but to the American people, the actions of the liberal judges who refused to recognize evidence presented by the Trump team and other conservative groups of the outright fraud at the polls. This shows the quality of judges we have in many of our courts. Many of them rule, not by law but by their political stance. I'm afraid our Supreme Court is badly infested with them also.

On January 6, 2021 a lot of people gathered in DC to protest; to voice their opinions on the fraudulent way the election had been conducted. Most were patriotic Americans exercising their First Amendment rights and their God-given rights and they announced several days in advance they would be there to protest and to show support for the man who actually won the election, Donald J. Trump.

Of course, by announcing their intent to protest, it gave the enemy time to prepare. Many people are convinced that the hoodlums doing the damage, anarchy if you will, were ANTIFA plants put there for the sole purpose of making the peaceful protesters look bad.

The left-wingers, the Pislosi's, the Schumers and the other true radicals are still mouthing about it and trying to blame President Trump. "Never miss an opportunity presented by a crisis". They tried to make it look like *every* person there was guilty of anarchy.

It's amazing how the socialist accuse conservative groups of the very things they are guiltiest of. Lying and cheating. It's what, in the world of psychiatry, is known as *transference*. Transferring one's own psychological or mental problems to someone else.

On January 10, 2021 the left-wing news channels, in their constant criticism of the January 6 protest march on Congress badly distorted the facts (as usual).

One commentator stated "five times as many arrests were made on the Black Lives Matter participants as were made during the protest in DC." He went on to say "The event on January 6 was an assault on democracy." Anything contrary to what they want, they consider against democracy or un-American.

To begin with, the escapades of the BLM and ANTIFA groups lasted for months. Throughout the summer, and some of their events are still happening, even though the people they worship managed to steal the election.

Most of their little get-togethers were quite violent, with windows being broken, businesses being looted and burned and people, including police, being attacked.

Of course none of these acts were considered an assault on democracy or even violent by the left-wing media or the socialist politicians. I recall seeing one newscast where the reporter was talking about the mayhem going on behind him. He said *"for the most part, it's quite peaceful."*

The scene was a large group of people raising hell. Cars being damaged or destroyed and in the back-ground a large building was ablaze. Almost no arrests were made during any of this "peaceful violence." But, bail money was furnished by Kamala Harris and several other left-wingers for the few that were arrested.

They called the event in DC an attack on democracy. No. It was an attack on "socialism" and that's why the Obiden team was outraged. It was estimated that more than 100,000 people were there but the vandalism was perpetrated by little more than 100 people. ANTIFA plants???

Strange how the socialist can find worlds of criticism

for Americans exercising their First Amendment rights but could never bring themselves to criticize any of the violence, looting and burning all over the Country throughout most of the summer. They spoke of that as "peaceful protests."

The following is a list of reminders from my long-time friend Jack Percy.

Remember in 2011 when tens of thousands of democrats surged on the Wisconsin Capitol building in Madison and physically occupied it for more than a week? We were told **"This is what democracy looks like."**

Remember in 2016 when Obama was President and hundreds of BLM blocked interstate highways and violently accosted police (even killing several)? We were told **"To assign the actions of one person to an entire movement is dangerous and irresponsible."**

Remember in 2018 during the Kavanaugh hearings when a mob of democrats stormed the U.S. Supreme Court building in Washington, DC and pounded their fists in rage on the door? We were told **"It's understandable."**

Remember this summer's riots in major cities across the country when groups of democrats marched in the streets, set buildings afire, looted businesses, assaulted and even killed bystanders and police? We were told **"These are mostly peaceful protests."**

Remember when democrats seized several blocks of the Capitol Hill neighborhood in downtown Seattle, declaring it an autonomous zone? Remember the guns and deaths *and utter destruction? We were told **"It's a block party atmosphere."***

*Remember when a crazed mob gathered after the Republican National Convention and attacked Rand Paul, a U.S. Senator? We were told **"No justice, no peace."***

*Remember how police were told to stand down, governors refused to call in the National Guard and democrats paid bail for violent protesters who were arrested? We were told **"This is the only way oppressed people can be heard."***

(Emphasis added).

It's now January 18, 2021 and it appears that, in two days, our great Nation will be turned over to the enemy from within; the first socialist regime in America. Already they are making plans for putting us in bondage, through exorbitant taxes, loss of jobs, canceling all improvements made by President Trump, and initiating more crippling and controlling laws. I fear our rights, freedoms and liberties will be lost forever.

These invaders from within have, for many months, talked about the huge changes they will make. They have made it quite clear they "will change America". Sadly, the people in our government ignored their threats. Most democrats of today seem to be in complete favor of socialism and too many republicans were too complacent, or lazy, to act.

It's true the denizens of the swamp hate President Trump because he has tried very hard to do what's best for America and the people. The "swamp rats" have become quite wealthy off the working people, but I find it impossible to understand how anyone born in this great land, can sit idly by and allow it to become a socialist nation.

The new regime will consist of an aged, doddering old fool that has difficulty completing a sentence and needs assistance to walk off the stage after trying to make a speech. My prediction is, he is being used as just a stepping-stone, a free ticket into the White House. He will probably *voluntarily* step aside after a few months for "health reasons" or will suffer a heart attack or other debilitating ailment. No doubt President Trump will be blamed.

In such an event, the de facto president, Kamala Harris, would take over. When this happens she will, no doubt, nominate Nancy Pelosi as *her* VP. That would be a nightmare beyond belief. That would be like having Hitler and Mussolini in charge.

Today's news report said the National guard troops being sent to DC for inaugural day are being "vetted" to make sure they will uphold the Constitution. Can anyone believe such an insult to our military? These are young men and women in service to our Nation who have sworn an oath when entering the service and are willing to go to war to protect us.

Yet, no one has vetted Joe Hussein Obiden and *Kamel* Harris as to where they stand on the Constitution. But, then, it really isn't necessary to ask them. They have talked (bragged), about the unconstitutional things they plan to do once they have stolen the White House. Of course they won't hesitate to turn the force of our patriotic military men and women on equally patriotic citizens who are trying to save our great Nation from the destruction of these socialist. The job our political leaders, military leaders and federal law-enforcement should have done.

These two usurpers will stand on inaugural day and tell a bold-faced lie when they take the oath of office as stated in Article II, section I of "our Constitution" which says *"I do solemnly swear (or affirm) that I will faithfully execute the office of President of the United States, and will, to the best of my ability, **preserve**, **protect** and **defend** the Constitution of the United States."*

Article II says nothing about destroying the Constitution...... as they plan.

INAUGURATION DAY

January 20, 2021

TODAY AMERICA SURRENDERED! After conducting the most fraudulent election in the history of America the socialist, the enemy within our own borders, stole our White House and our Nation. And no one had the courage to resist them, except the true, patriotic Americans; the Christian, working class people who were not allowed near the phony proceedings.

The new regime had the entire area fenced off with razor wire, like the confines of a prison, and brought in thousands of military, law enforcement and other security personnel. I'm not sure if this was to keep out the true Americans, who had every right to be there, or if it was to keep in any of their own who might change their minds, Perhaps both.

The size and number of their security force was an indication of the fear they felt, (I would say guilt if they were capable of such). The figure I heard was approximately twenty-five thousand.

Again this brings up the question I have wondered about since the last fake president was in office for eight years. "When any regime starts eliminating our Constitution, as these trespassers are set on doing, can we rely on our military and law enforcement to step up and fulfill their oath of office, or will they actually be willing to use the force of our own protectors against us? It's a frightening thought.

If such an event occurs, the leaders who give orders for our military or law enforcement to attack any patriotic citizens who try to resist these socialist, will no doubt, say "I was doing my duty. I was following orders." The same excuses many of the Nazi leaders used at the end of WWII after killing millions of people and causing mass destruction in many countries. Including Germany. Maybe we need a full regiment of "John Waynes". Or just assign Navy Seals to the task.

Doing one's duty or following orders is never an excuse for doing evil. Every member of our military and our law enforcement has sworn an oath to uphold and defend the Constitution. To protect and serve. I never knew one person in either job that didn't mean every word of the oath. It remains to be seen how many have forgotten their oath as they have advanced in rank.

On his first day of illegal occupation of the White House Obiden started putting his plan of action to work with, so-called, executive orders. He stopped work on the badly needed border wall to allow in the thousands of illegals who were already on the way in (at his invitation). He had made it known that they were welcome. (More socialist democrat votes). He also shut down work on the Keystone Pipeline putting thousands out of work. He had announced his intention to do so and gas prices started going up as soon as it appeared he would be able to complete his theft of the White House.

In his book "Jerusalem" Jay Sekulow used a phrase that is quite appropriate in Biden's case *"ex injuria jus non oritur"* meaning "illegal acts cannot create law." So true.

This puppet pretending to be a President is being directed and controlled by his socialist handlers. As one conservative newscaster put it, "this is Obama's third term." So far it's one destructive act after another. Every effort is to cancel or eradicate all the good things accomplished by President Trump. Which were many. It won't take four years for them to wipe it all out. So far most of his actions seem to be more for the benefit his friends, the Chinese, than for the American people.

Many people lost their jobs and now face higher prices (inflation) on almost everything, from gasoline, which has increased more than a dollar per gallon, to our food and clothing. The foolish (stupid) acts done by the "usurper-in-chief" have caused a chain reaction in the economy.

The so-called "stimulus checks", implying they are to stimulate the economy, are being sent out by the thousands with no thought as to whether some people don't need them. Such payments should have gone to people who lost their jobs and the small businesses that were struggling to remain open. People receiving some type of retirement can make it (if prices were not going out-of-sight). People already getting all their government handouts (welfare, food stamps, etc, etc.) will be fine. These people, retirees and welfare recipients did not suffer a loss of income. It's true, many people found the stimulus to be helpful but it was not needed to survive.

By putting people out of work, they have created a need for more unemployment checks, which they seem happy to provide. Now it appears people are being *paid* to stay home. As a result of this socialist generosity many companies cannot find people willing to work. Even the local Walmart can't get enough cashiers. The local restaurants can't get enough waiters and waitresses to serve the customers now that they are allowed to be open for normal operation again.

Even some of those who are willing to hold down a job and receive a paycheck don't seem to care if they do the job they were hired to do. A young man we have known since he was a child works at a local facility of a world-wide corporation. He related a situation there in which any employee can sleep on the job. When he reports it to his supervisor, the supervisor just says *"oh well, let him sleep until he wakes up and have him do this job."* The individual is allowed to sleep on the job and still have a job." Obviously some people feel that Uncle Joe will protect them from any repercussions.

We can but wonder how much of our tax dollar is going to the illegal aliens that have been allowed to swarm into the Country for all the freebies.

Of course the socialist answer to all this expense is to crank up the printing presses for more legal counterfeiting, and then raise taxes. This is all part of the socialists' scheme to bankrupt America, put people out of work and make them dependent on government. Next comes outright slavery. A society like they now have in Venezuela, New Zealand and some others.

For some time now, there has been talk among some of the socialist, of doing away with the U.S. dollar, which has served as the world's standard for a long time. Even Obama seemed to be eyeing the adaptation of the Euro, so popular in third world nations. Another idea is to make every monetary transaction digital.

Your paycheck will be electronic, direct deposit. You will be required to have a bank account. This will probably be paid for by the government for certain people. You will be required to have a debit/credit card for any transaction. You won't be able to drop a twenty in your grandchild's birthday card. To lend ten bucks to a friend you will have to *lend* them your debit card along with your pin number.

The reasoning behind such a move, besides control, is to keep track of every dime that comes into your possession so you can be taxed on it. They can also make sure the deadbeats have as much as you, even though they refuse to work for it (guaranteed income).

Obiden and his nest of rattlesnakes, are spending like drunken sailors on payday. Unfortunately, they are spending on things that serve no benefit to the Nation nor the taxpayer...only to buy votes. Open borders. Free everything. There is nothing more devious, more conniving, than the criminal mind.

The left-wing media, along with the brainwashing of our young people, have convinced a lot of the population that they have been cheated; that the government owes them anything their little heart desires. The Hollywood elite have joined forces with them.

In November 1947, the House On UnAmerican Activities Committee (HUAC) cited ten people in Tinsel Town for refusing to answer questions or co-operate in hearings pertaining to communism in the movie industry. They became known as "The Hollywood Ten." J. Parnell Thomas, HUAC Chairman, told the people *"The Constitution was never intended to cloak or shield those who would destroy it."*

These trials, or hearings, were debated for many years and the more they were discussed, the more the accusers were criticized and condemned. The very Constitution they were trying so hard to protect, was used against them.

After more than seventy years, it's difficult to say if any of the accused were guilty of being communist but one might consider the old saying "where there's smoke, there's fire." There must have been something to invite an investigation.

Whether or not any of the "Hollywood Ten" were communist, their denial turned into a rallying cry, much like BLM. An all-out effort by the socialist. They tripled their efforts using every means possible to influence the young people, and they had the perfect tools with which to work. The media and our schools.

In the first half of the twentieth century most stars in Hollywood were true, patriotic Americans, The story-lines were about things that made America great; good vs evil. Crime doesn't pay During WWII, many of the biggest stars put their careers on hold and joined the military. Today's stars would probably join the other side.

People like Clark Gable, who flew missions over Germany and made training films to train new pilots.

Gene Autry, the most popular singing cowboy at the time, became a pilot flying troops and supplies in a C-47 (DC-3). A dangerous assignment because the cargo planes were not armed.

A lot of the stars were past the age to participate and found other ways to help. There were War Bond drives. Some found time to entertain the troops in places like the Hollywood Canteen. Some even went into combat zones to entertain, Folks like Bob Hope, Frances Langford and Jerry Colona as well as others. Others only became famous after the war, eg. Lee Marvin, Bob Keeshan (Captain Kangaroo), Eddie Albert (Green Acres) all decorated heroes. The most highly decorated soldier of WWII was Audie Murphy, who became famous as a cowboy star. He was originally from Texas.

So many of today's "Hollywood Elite" are part of the enemy force and propaganda machine. Of course the only requirement to become a star today is to take off their clothes and talk filth.

Many, if not most, in Hollywood are in complete agreement with the socialist, giving support to BLM and ANTIFA, while these groups are out rioting and destroying cities, yelling "de-fund the police."

When people of my generation were growing up, we had a lot of, patriotic models to look up to. Real heroes, both movie stars and sports figures. Not drug addicts like so many today.

Today's movies are, not only violent but, contain more filth and trash than a fungus factory. They have even found ways to turn comic books into pornography. As a child I loved the comics; all books, but they contained no lewdness. They were adventure stories along with art. I drew many of the comic characters in school when I was supposed to be studying. I shouldn't tell my grandchildren that.

Hollywood has taken the classic comics and turned them into filth. Recently I started watching a "modern" movie titled *"Batman vs Superman."* After about ten minutes or so I changed channels. It's no wonder so many of our young people have no morals. The movies of my youth just had better actors *and* better writers.

It now seems that vulgarity is considered "free speech" along with burning the American flag and "taking a knee" for the National Anthem. Of course this is one of the socialist interpretations to destroy the morals of our young people. This is all permissible but prayer is not allowed any place.

By "Free Speech" most Americans interpret that part of the First Amendment to mean the right to complain, voice our opinions and even criticize our elected leaders. The question now becomes "How long will any such free speech last under a socialist regime? Especially if they eliminate the Second Amendment, because, right now, the Second Amendment is the only thing protecting the First Amendment. I fear we are about to lose both.

On March 16, 2021, the National News reported on a mother and daughter arrested in Florida for "fraudulently" getting the daughter elected as homecoming queen. If convicted, the report said, they could be sentenced to a hefty fine and up to six years in prison.

The mother is the principal of the school and

manipulated the school's computer to give her daughter extra, undeserved votes.

Does this scenario sound somewhat familiar? Sounds very much like the mother took lessons from the 2020 Presidential election in which Joe Biden and Kamala Harris managed to steal the election, the White House and the Nation.

While the crime committed by this mother and daughter was thoughtless, inconsiderate and mean, it was an act that will probably not be remembered a year from now. But, the theft committed by Biden and his socialist handlers affected our entire Nation and, no doubt, will for years to come. Perhaps even for our great-grandchildren, and yet, no action was taken against them. Was their crime less severe than the mother and daughter in Florida? I think not. I ask again "where were our military and law enforcement?"

As I have stated, several times, I consider our Constitution to be the greatest document ever conceived, after the Holy Bible. But, I have felt for many years now, that it can also be our downfall, because it protects our enemies in our midst just as it protects us. They have now proven that fact.

Those enemies within our borders, both foreign and home-grown, have learned to use our Constitution and our laws to their advantage while denying us the same rights. They never sleep.

EPILOGUE

Our nation is truly in crisis. This could very well be the generation Ronald Reagan spoke of when he said "Freedom is never more than one generation away from extinction". I fear, that for too many years, we have not heard the chains being forged, and it may be too late for us to reverse our captivity.

For several generations now, the bonds have been made tighter and tighter. People have been too busy just trying to make a living and have not noticed. We have not paid attention to some of the propaganda being disseminated in our schools and our children have been taught that our country is evil and has been throughout history. Perhaps it's why an individual of questionable citizenship, and obvious intent, was allowed to occupy the White House for eight years.

Obama was allowed to hold the highest office in the world without *proving* his origin, and yet, when I went recently to renew my driver's license I took several pieces of ID, including the license that was about to expire. I intended to get the new one called "the REAL ID". I had my original birth certificate, that I had shown when I entered the U.S. military and obtained a top secret clearance (Army Security Agency), my DD214 from my time in service and a utility bill. The birth certificate was issued by my home state, eighty-five years ago, where I currently reside, and was trying to get the new-fangled license. The same birth certificate and DD214. I had used to become a police officer for a major metropolitan city, as well as other jobs I have held in my lifetime. I was told these pieces of ID were not valid and I would have to get certified copies, which I could obtain at the county health department. At a cost, of course. (Revenue). Maybe I should have run for president. It worked for Obama.

It appears the socialist now feel they have enough people brainwashed and are in a position to totally get rid of anyone who has any patriotism or believes in God. When they can have such a large percentage of the population believing their socialist crap and have come to the point of actually hating the country, I'm sure it gives them a tremendous amount of confidence.

It's bad enough that we have allowed so many people to enter the country who, obviously, hate us but the sad part is the number of people who were born here and should have a degree of love and respect for America, that are working so hard to destroy the nation.

These subversive groups have convinced the young people to be destructive, by promising all sorts of freebies. They are now involved in anarchy and social unrest. They have been convinced that so many symbols of history are bad and must *all* be destroyed. They are tearing down statues and any kind of memorials having anything to do with America's history. These things are just that, symbols of history. Obviously most of these people have never heard the statement "he who fails to observe history is bound to repeat it". They are now Wanting to remove even statues or other symbols of Jesus Christ. I'm afraid the socialists are in charge.

People are not being taught any morals or respect for anyone or anything. I saw a face-book photo of an old statue and an individual with his pants down almost past his butt. The caption asks the question "how can a statue that has been there for a hundred years be offensive, and yet the individual exposing his rear end is *not* offensive"? No doubt these same offensive people who allow their pants to drag out their tracks expect to be treated with *respect*. But this is how so many are being trained under the new world order.

Thanks to our socialist invaders, everything real and decent is being destroyed at a rapid pace and I think it's time the Christian people learn some of the guerilla tactics being used by the subversives. Does that sound "politically incorrect? That's too bad. Political correctness has been one of their weapons for some time now.

If anyone is offended by these writings, please don't wait for an apology from me. I have been offended for some time by the obvious efforts of people, who should have some pride in America, doing anything they can to bring her down. I don't think I am the only one who feels this way. I just hope a lot of people, who have been lax in their thoughts and actions, will wake up and decide to start voicing their opinions.

Let's not forget what has been sacrificed by our

founding fathers, all the brave men who gave us our freedom and independence. Let's not forget the many men and women who have fought and died to keep America free and those still making the sacrifice today.

It's time for every true, freedom-loving American to shout from every hill top, roof top and street corner, "this land is my land and I will, with God's help, defend her from *all* enemies. "One nation, under God".

GOD BLESS AMERICA

Home of the Free
Because of the Brave

America, *please* wake up.

Printed in the United States
by Baker & Taylor Publisher Services